THE CATALYST EFFECT

12 Skills and Behaviors to Boost Your Impact and Elevate Team Performance

The Catalyst Effect cuts straight to the chase on what it takes to be a true leader through collective trust and empowerment. When one chooses to give up their own personal victory for the progression of the team, the results are powerful and real. This book shows you how. A superbly inspiring read!

> — *Stephen M. R. Covey, The New York Times and*
> *# 1 Wall Street Journal bestselling author of*
> *The SPEED of Trust and coauthor of Smart Trust*

I truly love the ideas in the book. Thoroughly researched and full of practical suggestions, *The Catalyst Effect* lights the path for every person in every organization to see themselves as leaders. It shows us that everyone is a leader and can get better at leading, if they recognize that truth.

> — *Angela Duckworth, Founder and CEO, Character Lab,*
> *Christopher H. Browne Distinguished Professor of Psychology,*
> *and bestselling author of GRIT*

When Yo-Yo Ma brought together master musicians from different cultures to form The Silk Road Ensemble, he sought to instill a unique sound and a cohesive spirit. I have had the privilege of being part of the Ensemble and experiencing performances that achieve heights beyond our dreams.

The Catalyst Effect engagingly describes the leadership and teamwork principles that bring his vision to life. Through Yo-Yo's natural style, he embodies the ideas presented in this book. *The Catalyst Effect* shows how these skills and behaviors can be applied in all types of organizations to produce superb results.

> — *Sandeep Das, Tabla player and composer, collaborator with*
> *Yo-Yo Ma for the Silk Road Ensemble,*
> *Grammy Award Winner*

The Catalyst Effect is at once inspirational and pragmatic. The authors offer a fresh perspective of what teamwork and leadership can look like in flatter organizations. Through the rare combination of a strong narrative and solid research, the authors deliver the insights and tools needed to lead, regardless of his or her formal title. Each of us can learn something from this book. I did.

> — *Daniel H. Pink, Author of DRIVE and TO SELL IS HUMAN*

With society seeming more fragmented and divided, the responsibility of leaders to bring people together to accomplish great things can be more difficult than ever before. *The Catalyst Effect* is a practical primer to help all leaders inspire teamwork and collaboration to boost team performance and achieve great results.

> — *Bill Stanczykiewicz, Director, The Fund Raising School,*
> *Senior Lecturer, Philanthropic Studies,*
> *IU Lilly Family School of Philanthropy*

The Catalyst Effect competencies fit hand-in-glove with Servant Leadership principles. The model invites readers, whether they are in informal or formal leadership roles, to identify and develop the key skills that will increase their effectiveness and impact.

> — *Pat Falotico, CEO,*
> *Robert K. Greenleaf Center for Servant Leadership®*

Some leaders are viewed as solitary gems. They outshine their peers with an intense luminosity that makes them stand apart. That view, however, may be erroneous or at least incomplete, according to Jerry Toomer, Craig Caldwell, Steve Weitzenkorn, and Chelsea Clark, authors of *The Catalyst Effect*. The writers argue that some of the most impactful leaders succeed by elevating the performance of their team, by making not just the solitary gem but the entire necklace dazzle. *The Catalyst Effect* highlights a dozen competencies that anyone can cultivate to become better at catalyzing leadership and teamwork. Whether you are a leader or a team member, you will learn a lot from this book.

> — *Mukul Pandya, Editor-in-Chief, Knowledge@Wharton*

The best leaders and colleagues have something in common: they make everyone around them better. This is a hands-on playbook for building that capability in your team.

> — *Adam Grant, New York Times bestselling*
> *author of GIVE AND TAKE, ORIGINALS,*
> *and OPTION B with Sheryl Sandberg*

The Catalyst Effect has given me a number of useful tools and new approaches in leading my organization and civic partnerships and in supporting my teammates as they lead. I also believe it will be a big help to my college-student son as he prepares to find his way in his career. The book's framework makes it very easy to review the most important advice and relevant wisdom in each leadership situation and for each individual. I highly recommend it.

— *Brian Payne, President and CEO of the Central Indiana Community Foundation and the Founder of the Indianapolis Cultural Trail*

The Catalyst Effect illuminates the elements of leadership that are essential in any successful ensemble endeavor — in business, sports and certainly in the arts. Outstanding orchestra performances require each individual to focus on the team goal, understand when to lead and when to follow and uphold a standard of excellence that inspires their colleagues and their audience. This book provides incredible insight into the way these key concepts apply across sectors and what they look like in practice.

— *Gary Ginstling, Executive Director, National Symphony Orchestra, Artistic Affiliate of the John F. Kennedy Center for the Performing Arts*

What is important is not a formal title, but how you impact your teams and your organization as a catalyst from wherever you are. The authors skillfully blend real life examples from business, sports and not for profit organizations with sound research in a highly readable manner. You will learn the "why, what and how" of being a catalytic leader.

This is a highly valuable book for professionals and leaders at all levels who work in teams across different settings and cultures!

— *Julie Fasone-Holder, CEO JFH Insights, Independent Board Member, Retired SVP Dow Chemical*

Building successful groups rarely happens by chance. It takes wisdom. This book offers such wisdom by focusing on specific skills that team members can develop to enhance each other's success, thereby enhancing overall team performance. Catalytic leadership makes the whole much more than the sum of its parts.

— *Hersh Shefrin, Mario Belotti Professor, Santa Clara University*

At a time when the social contract between employer and employee is changing, *The Catalyst Effect* provides a valuable perspective on how employee engagement can thrive. Investing in *everyone's* ability to lead at the appropriate time in team settings can foster a vibrant culture and drive impact. The book is filled with ideas for application and was a pleasure to read.

— Bryan Adkins, CEO, Denison Consulting

The authors have brilliantly uncovered a powerful component of team structure, appropriately coined it "catalyst," and provided a great guide to apply the concept. The catalyst concept coupled with strong leadership cannot deliver anything but powerful results. Effectively and clearly written with colorful and real life examples to supplement the concept, this is a must read for those interested in leading from wherever they are. I will recommend this book to all I know, not just in the business world.

— Wahida Saeedi, Global Finance Leader,
Pharmaceutical Industry

The Catalyst Effect is fun, engaging, insightful, theoretically sound, highly useful, and my new favorite leadership book! I can't wait to use it in my leadership class next semester. When it comes to books for people who aspire to high levels of impact in an organization, but don't have a fancy title, *The Catalyst Effect* fills a void. Whether used as a reading in a university course, material to develop young professionals, or as a guide to show senior leaders how to identify hidden catalysts in their organization, the lessons in this book will prove incredibly valuable.

— Bradley R. Agle, George W. Romney Endowed Professor,
Marriott School of Management, Brigham Young University

Some people simply help their colleagues perform better — often in ways that have been difficult to measure and cultivate in the past. This book is a giant step toward identifying and proliferating the catalytic capabilities that can make every organization more successful.

— Thomas H. Davenport, Distinguished Professor, Babson College and
Digital Fellow, MIT Initiative on the Digital Economy, and
author of Competing on Analytics and Only Humans Need Apply

THE CATALYST EFFECT

12 Skills and Behaviors to Boost Your Impact and Elevate Team Performance

BY

JERRY TOOMER
CRAIG CALDWELL
STEVE WEITZENKORN
CHELSEA CLARK

United Kingdom – North America – Japan
India – Malaysia – China

Emerald Publishing Limited
Howard House, Wagon Lane, Bingley BD16 1WA, UK

First edition 2018

Reprints and permissions service
Contact: permissions@emeraldinsight.com

British Library Cataloguing in Publication Data
A catalogue record for this book is available from the British Library

ISBN: 978-1-78743-552-0 (Print)
ISBN: 978-1-78743-551-3 (Online)
ISBN: 978-1-78743-568-1 (Epub)
ISBN: 978-1-78754-811-4 (Paperback)

ISOQAR certified
Management System,
awarded to Emerald
for adherence to
Environmental
standard
ISO 14001:2004.

Certificate Number 1985
ISO 14001

INVESTOR IN PEOPLE

This book is passionately written for the catalysts —
the glue-guys and gals who make their teams better by
leading from the middle

CONTENTS

ACKNOWLEDGMENTS

Behind each book is a story. There is a spark of an idea; a personal experience; a powerful feeling that generates the motivation to share ideas with others, and ultimately to write them down.

The idea for our field research and the book was sparked by the notion of the no-stats all-star. As an athlete and as an ultimate team performer, Shane Battier made others around him better when he stepped on the court. We were curious. If we explored this idea with professionals and leaders in different organizations beyond sports, what would we hear?

"Do you know someone who when they step on the court or the field or into the conference room or onto the stage makes everyone around them better, and if yes, what is it that they do? Describe this as specifically as you can."

What we heard from 80+ interviews with individuals across sports, business, and the arts provided the raw input for the identification of the 4 cornerstones and 12 competencies. There was validation and a level of consistency in what we heard.

Our personal experiences also validated the idea as we have played on sports teams, participated in choirs and ensembles, and been members of teams in a wide variety of work and volunteer settings. Each of us could point to times when a team was better because of a catalytic member. As we scanned the literature we also saw an ample number of leadership articles and books that were written from the perspective of someone with formal authority: we saw a need for further exploration of how people "lead from the middle" rather than from the top.

We also closely tied the approach to teamwork and leadership at Butler University called The Butler Way, which is very consistent with the cornerstones and competencies we have identified in our field research.

So with the spark of the idea, the passion from our personal experiences, and the motivation to share the ideas with others, we embarked on a several years' long journey of field research and writing.

Brad Stevens, then Butler's men's basketball coach, provided initial encouragement and input. His early thumbs-up regarding the idea of the "catalyst" was key to our decision to dive into the interview process. And his continuing counsel and support in the midst of his demanding schedule has made our work better. Beth Perdue Outland of the Indianapolis Symphony Orchestra added creatively to our early thinking and the field interview question set, and she made available several members of the orchestra and the ISO staff. Lee Dicklitch, a Butler MBA program graduate and Indy area sports leader, has been invaluable during the entire life of the project and the writing process. His continuing willingness to partner with us on research, interviews, and website ideas is a gift.

Most importantly, we found a wonderful developmental editor. Jeanne Glasser Levine is everything you hope for in a writing partner. She "gets it" and is passionate about our catalyst effect ideas. Her deep experience in publishing provided a roadmap by which we navigated the final year of writing, and her writing skills and easy working style make her both catalytic and appropriately tough on a gaggle of four authors!

— Jerry, Craig, Steve, and Chelsea

Two threads in my life have come together in this book. The first relates to my experience as a high school and college athlete when I played for teams both good and bad. Some of the teams struggled mightily and experienced little success. Some of the teams went about their work in a low-key, professional, and enjoyable manner. They regularly competed for victories and championships. As I was finishing my Ph.D. at Pitt and beginning to work at Butler University, the Butler men's basketball team enjoyed what was becoming a trend, shocking victories over larger schools. The victories over supposedly better teams happened so often that it challenged my thoughts about luck and random chance.

At about the same time, I was honing my skills teaching leadership. Early in my teaching experience, I loaded the readings packet with cases about top CEOs. This was and is a common practice. However, I began sensing a disconnect between what I was teaching and the kind of opportunities MBA students were likely to experience in the next five to ten years.

When Jerry Toomer and I began exploring an article on Shane Battier in *The New York Times*, I did not know that I would find a potential explanation to the organizational success questions that came from my earlier years in sports, *and* an approach to leadership that was much more relevant and hopeful for my MBA students. The phenomenon was catalytic leadership.

For me, catalytic leadership can provide teams and organizations with the missing ingredient for success. It can also offer leadership tools to a 28-year-old MBA, seeking to impact her organization without the advantage of being the CEO.

I would like to thank a consistent supporter of this project, Brad Stevens. I appreciate his advice and friendship. When Brad left Butler University to coach the Boston Celtics, I said goodbye and thank you, not really expecting to have much contact with him beyond that. As a person who really lives his values, he still makes time for me, despite the crushing demands of an NBA coach.

My parents, Carl and Carolyn, deserve a hearty thank you. They endured years of my academic mediocrity while I tried to divine the purpose of working hard in school. My children (Maya, Talia, and Elena) also deserve a hearty thank you as the last year of work on this book has eaten into time that might normally be dedicated to them. The upside is that the book has given us much to talk about as we have explored these ideas together.

Last and most important, I have enjoyed the unwavering support, affirmation, and love of my wife, Diana. She is, unlike me, a uniquely optimistic, hopeful, and positive person. Those qualities, as well as being witness to her wildly productive ways, have changed my opinion about how good people should act and what they can accomplish.

— Craig Caldwell

I am very grateful for the love, support, and inspiration of my wife, Bonnie Kabin, throughout this project and all other times. My contributions to this endeavor were only possible because of the many great colleagues, teachers, advisors, friends, and clients from whom I have learned over the years. Many were excellent role models. Most shared their wisdom and expertise generously. All helped me to learn, grow, and become adept at applying my capabilities to help others — and their organizations — be more successful. I humbly thank them all for enriching my life and career.

— Steve Weitzenkorn

Producing this book has certainly been a team effort! I would like to begin by thanking Dr. Jerry Toomer and Dr. Craig Caldwell for inviting me to join this project, first as a research associate and then as a coauthor. If not for their original interest in the concept of the no-stats all-star, I wouldn't have had the opportunity to explore the concepts of leadership and teamwork so deeply. Additionally, I am incredibly grateful to my dissertation advisor, Dr. Tom Carsey, who taught me how to be both a good researcher and a good person — one who gives back and *pays it forward*. Thanks to my husband, Phillip — who has been a constant source of support and motivation as I've worked on this book project. Thanks to his parents, my in-laws, who have shown a keen interest in my research and encouraged me throughout the process. Thanks to my parents — who always believed I could do anything I set my mind to and encouraged me to pursue my passions. Most importantly, I thank my Lord and Savior Jesus Christ, who created me with specific abilities and endowed me with unique talents, which allowed me to serve the research team and the aims of this project.

— Chelsea Clark

Thanks to Linda, Chris, and Winda (Setyaweni) Toomer for their continuing love and support of my work and career over the past many years.

I'm also grateful for the encouragement and input from many wise people over the years: key mentors, coaches, conductors, colleagues, precocious students, and, of course, our 80+ interviewees. Without them this book would not have been conceived or written.

In addition to the people mentioned above, there were contributors, aka catalysts, for the stories and callouts in the book. Thanks to each of you!

David Armstrong	Carl Heck
Shane Battier	Linda Hajduk
Alan Bowers	Austin Hastings
Barry Collier	Tom Jernestedt
Annette Coulumbe	Stephanie Judge
Sandeep Das	Lisa Reiser
Bettye Ellison	JoAn Scott
Bill Fanelli	Matt Tanner
Janet Giesselman	Jim Thorne

— Jerry Toomer

FOREWORD

As a student at DePauw University, I took a class called, "Servant Leadership." It was tremendously impactful and introduced me to the idea of leading by serving others. Up to that point, I had always been under the impression that all leaders were strong-willed, vocal, and had an undeniable presence in the room. But after that class, it all started to make a little more sense — the true leaders were the ones that were empowering others, often out of the limelight. We learned that anyone in an organization can empower coworkers or teammates, so ultimately everyone in an organization has a leadership responsibility to do just that.

After graduating from college and completing a brief stint as a marketing associate at Eli Lilly in Indianapolis, I kicked off my coaching career at Butler University. Every day of the 13 years that I was there, someone would ask me, "What makes Butler so special?" The simple answer is the people. The administration has always done an exceptional job of creating an environment where employees are both aligned and empowered. The faculty and staff are committed to teaching, leading, and challenging the students to think not only about what they want to do with their lives, but how they can impact the lives of others. And, the students inspired us all to think daily about the best ways to maximize their intellect, creativity, ambition, and commitment to working together as a broader community. At Butler, service to others was a big part of the fabric of the school, and there were many great examples of servant leaders.

In 2009, two professors in our Lacy School of Business, Jerry Toomer and Craig Caldwell, wanted to talk about an article that they had read in *The New York Times*. The article was about NBA player, Shane Battier, and his unique impact on the court, despite the fact that he was considered to be more of a role player than a star. The article was very insightful, and not only illustrated Shane's value as a basketball player but also gave fans of the game a greater insight into the use of analytics that consistently impacted decisions made by their favorite teams.

We met and discussed the article and some of the corresponding research they had begun conducting. As they researched the "Battier Effect" in sports, business, and the arts, three things became very clear to me. First, it was hard to find organizations that viewed leadership as a collective responsibility, instead of a task shared by a chosen few. Second, it was clear that Shane Battier, and others like him, were truly unique in their willingness to fully embrace their role, whatever it may be, for the good of the whole. And finally (and ironically), we found ourselves at a point in time with the Butler Basketball program where we had a group of these players on one team, at one time. The more we talked, the more I realized we had something truly special, and it was our job to take advantage of it.

Over the next couple of years, our staff spent a lot of time thinking about how we could promote "catalytic leadership" over more traditional forms of leadership. We debated the need for team captains. We talked even more about the importance of clearly defining roles that fit the strengths of each of our players. Like every other team, we had always emphasized the characteristics shared by catalysts — embracing that role, doing your job well, and putting the team above self. We always wanted to have 15 players doing that, but we had never thought of that in terms of having 15 *authentic leaders*.

After hearing Craig present his research over the years to prospective athletes wanting to major in business (I probably wore him out with all of the campus visits we asked him to participate in), we invited him to speak to our team in the fall semester of the 2012–2013 school year. As is usually the case, we were looking for something that our team could latch onto at the start of October that would be with us throughout the entire season. We knew that Craig's message would immediately resonate, and when he used the phrase "catalytic leadership," we knew we had something that would last. The next day we made t-shirts for our players. On the front of those t-shirts was our typical Bulldog logo. On the back was one word: CATALYST. It would serve throughout the season as a reminder that we shared ownership and were responsible to fulfill our role for each other.

We are all responsible for the health of the organizations we serve. I hope that you appreciate this book, as much as I appreciated all of the thought and research that Craig, Jerry, and their coauthors, Steve Weitzenkorn, and Chelsea Clark, invested in writing it.

Brad Stevens
Head Coach, Boston Celtics

PREFACE

The world is changing and it's changing fast. Leadership at all levels must keep pace.

Organizations are constantly adapting to new realities in technology, to worker sophistication and preferences, and global market pressures. By necessity, organizations have become flatter and leaner. These structural changes affect internal working relationships.

Leadership and teamwork must meet the challenges presented by this whirlwind of continual change — not just regarding these trends but also that workforces are evolving dramatically. They are experiencing greater diversity than ever before as well as growing generational and cultural differences. The challenge is to stay true to organizational values, align with overarching strategic objectives, and achieve specific team and individual goals. That's where catalytic leadership comes into play.

In a high-velocity world, this book reveals the *how* — the specific mindsets and competencies — for winning at individual, team, and organizational levels. How perspectives are broadened. How performance is heightened. How team effectiveness is improved. How team members who lead successfully without formal authority produce group decisions that maximize commitment, raise the performance of others, and ultimately generate higher-level results. This is what we call the "Catalyst Effect."

The Catalyst Effect is created by fusing leadership and teamwork into a dynamic, optimistic, and cohesive force that raises the performance of everyone involved and elevates overall team success.

The Catalyst Effect provides a practical, research-based roadmap for developing and applying 12 key competencies to multiply an individual's impact and drive progress toward team goals. We conducted over 80 in-depth interviews with highly successful professionals and leaders in business, sports, and the arts. Participants provided robust examples of catalytic leadership and teamwork in action. We then performed content and behavioral analyses that allowed us to isolate the 12 key competencies that comprise catalytic behavior. These examples are featured throughout the book, illustrating the impact of each competency and showing how to apply that particular skill.

WHAT CREATES A CATALYST EFFECT?

The Catalyst Effect is created by fusing leadership and teamwork into a dynamic, optimistic, and cohesive force that raises the performance of everyone involved and elevates overall team success. Being a catalytic leader or a catalytic teammate has little to do with official authority and everything to do with personal and professional credibility, putting the team and the pursuit of mission-oriented goals ahead of personal interests, and striving to elevate the performance of everyone you touch to accomplish big picture goals. It also has little to do with climbing career ladders, although catalysts may be prime candidates for creating value at higher levels.

> *When you master the jungle gym, you develop a broader range of competencies, greater agility, and the ability to fuse multiple skill sets.*

Catalytic leadership skills may be most effectively developed in flatter organizations by mastering what Tobi Lütke, the CEO of Shopify, calls "jungle gyms" rather than vertical career ladders (Bryant, 2016). When you master the jungle gym you develop a broader range of competencies, greater agility, and the ability to fuse multiple skill sets — and therefore gain greater ability to contribute and help others and your team in multiple ways. When you watch kids on jungle gyms, they often help and encourage each other. They offer tips. They catch friends when they lose their grip or fall off balance. You'll also see this at gymnastic camps. This is how trust is built and respect gained — which are essential building blocks of effective leadership and catalytic teamwork.

The 12 competencies are your catalytic jungle gym, each step bringing you higher and closer to behaving like a catalyst in your work life, on your teams, and in your personal endeavors. Each taken alone, the competencies may seem obvious, but become catalytic when they are used in combination and ultimately engrained in an individual's behavior. It is then that they inspire and enrich the performance of the entire group.

The path to becoming a catalytic teammate and leader begins here.

INTRODUCTION: CATALYTIC TEAMWORK IN ACTION

The NBA's Houston Rockets recognized catalytic teamwork in the play of Shane Battier. The *New York Times Magazine* called him "The No-Stats All-Star" (Lewis, 2009). The article sparked our interest. We wanted to know how Battier went from being a star in high school and college, to a relatively unheralded small forward and shooting guard for the Memphis Grizzlies, to ultimately a game-changing player. It began when he was traded to the Houston Rockets. There, Battier became a human catalyst. When he was on the court, his teammates played at a higher level, their performance metrics improved, and he elevated his team's competitiveness. Everything got better. How did he do it?

In an interview for this book, Shane said his original intention was not primarily to make others better. He simply focused on doing all he could to stay on the court. The Rocket's General Manager, Daryl Morey, explained that their analytics experts discovered the team performed better with Shane on the floor rather than on the bench. He did not put up huge numbers like the team's stars, but other players and the team posted even bigger numbers when he was part of the action.

The hallmark of catalytic teamwork and leadership is unselfishly making others better and heightening the team's ability to achieve results.

Our research reveals why Battier became such a dynamic force and team leader and what he and others like him have done in sports, the arts, business, and community organizations to create similar results. It is a

1

phenomenon that can be replicated. It involves a unique set of competencies that can be learned and applied by those with the desire, work ethic, and discipline to do so. Effective application of Catalyst Effect competencies increases your value to the team and the organization.

MULTIPLE CATALYSTS PROPEL PERFORMANCE

Leadership and catalytic teamwork are not easily measured but Battier's impact showed up on the scoreboard and in his teammates' stats. If one would look at his individual scoring stats, you might see nothing exceptional. His impact becomes obvious only when looking at the team as a whole and analyzing the performance of others. The hallmark of catalytic teamwork and leadership *is unselfishly making others better and heightening the team's ability to achieve results.* Combined, they allow teams and organizations to rise to extraordinary levels and out-compete teams richer in superstar talent.

The authors were struck by another catalytic phenomenon — one prompted by the amazing performance of the Butler University men's basketball teams. Coach Brad Stevens filled his roster with potential catalytic players. They were team-oriented athletes with strong work ethics and positive outlooks. Stevens steeped them in a culture that put the team first and rewarded players who helped each other succeed. By collegiate basketball standards, they were undersized and, by all outward appearances, should have been dominated by highly touted blue-blood programs. Yet they kept winning, driven by their catalytic practices and belief in themselves — and what they could make possible. Ultimately, they made it to back-to-back final games in the 2010 and 2011 NCAA Championship Tournament.

In sports, Shane Battier showed the impact one catalytic leader could have on a team. Brad Stevens and the Butler Bulldogs demonstrated the multiplied impact on performance when a team is built to include several catalysts.

WHY MANAGERS NEED CATALYSTS NOW MORE THAN EVER

In sports, you can see catalytic leadership and teamwork in action during the course of a game. In business, the arts, and community organizations, it's not so easy. But it's there and we uncovered it.

We started with the Indianapolis Symphony Orchestra. We discussed with members of a wind ensemble how it was that five people, all recognized as supremely talented on their own instruments, could come together as a unit. Without using our term, they described how they influenced each other catalytically, realizing that they had succeeded through their performance as an ensemble. We've witnessed this same phenomenon in companies and groups as diverse as a McDonald's restaurant to the Silk Road Ensemble. What's different about the people and organizations that embrace catalytic principles and skills?

> *Catalysts think beyond their immediate role to ensure what they do is aligned with the overall strategy.*

Team members that have a catalytic impact, think and act differently. In addition to doing their jobs well, they look at the bigger picture — at the overarching goals of their organization or team. In sports, they think like a coach. In business, they think like an executive. In a music ensemble, they focus on how the entire group sounds and how each player contributes to delighting the audience. They think like a conductor.

Catalysts think beyond their immediate role to ensure what they do is aligned with the overall strategy. They mentor in key moments to help those around them maintain a similar focus. They prioritize team performance and growth over personal accolades. Catalysts relish the hard work needed to overcome obstacles to success. Their combination of optimism and grit is contagious. They seldom fear failure or, if they do, they push through it. They quickly get off the mat when they fall and persevere through tough circumstances. Their example and determination advances the team and helps make everyone around them better. Like a chemical that accelerates reactions, they ignite higher levels of performance.

Developing catalytic leaders and team members has never been more important. Organizations have flattened their structures — they have *delayered.* More people report to fewer managers. This has been the case in nearly every traditional industry from automobile manufacturing to the chemical business to the tech sector. Much of this delayering took place in the middle levels and directly impacted supervisory and managerial positions. Significantly reduced layers sometimes resulted in a fivefold increase in the number of a manager's direct reports. Managers were no longer day-to-day team leaders who monitored operational goals, worked closely with each employee, and led daily work team meetings. Employees had to step up to take on these responsibilities with much greater autonomy. They had to develop and apply a broader set of competencies suited to these new circumstances.

Tony Hsieh, founder of Zappos Incorporation, an online retailer, spearheaded the idea of *no reporting layers at all*, which is an example of holacracy (Leinbach-Reyhle, 2014). Work was achieved via teams who collaborated around specific projects and achieved clear, specific results. This required nearly everyone in the organization to step up and lead when necessary on a given project or set of tasks. There were few individuals with any authority to direct the work from the top of the organization, rather, employees were asked to *lead from the middle* to move the team forward to deliver clear results.

In a holacracy, most employees have no specific boss. In less pure forms, there is still some hierarchical structure, but firms recognize the value of removing layers. Without bosses, people are expected to pursue, as an individual or team member, those initiatives that are consistent with the organization or the team's strategic plans.

In a less formally structured environment with very limited numbers of recognized bosses, catalytic leadership skills become even more critical because greater weight is placed on individual autonomy. Those who can lead by elevating or propelling individual and team performance have an outsized impact. When they lead catalytically, the enterprise moves faster and more effectively.

Catalytic leadership and teamwork competencies enable you to lead from wherever you are within an organization.

CATALYTIC LEADERSHIP AND TEAMWORK

In physical science, a catalyst causes a chemical transformation to develop faster. In the social sciences, a human catalyst accelerates action toward a goal. By blending the two definitions, we get to the crux of catalytic teamwork and leadership. *The Catalyst Effect phenomenon fuses leadership and teamwork into a dynamic, optimistic, and cohesive force that raises the performance of everyone involved and elevates overall team success.* Our definition embodies the transformational and action aspects of the physical and social sciences.

Leadership is about taking an endeavor, enterprise, or organization from one point to another. A catalytic leader accelerates progress toward common goals, including stimulating higher levels of performance among those engaged in the process.

Catalytic teamwork and leadership create value and heightens performance within the scope of one's own position. It's not about assuming authority without permission or undermining the authority of others. It requires alignment with the priorities of one's boss. We do not advocate assuming supervisory or managerial authority that has not been earned or granted. That is a prescription for conflict and dysfunction.

BECOMING A CATALYST: THE 12 CATALYTIC COMPETENCIES

Twelve competencies define the behaviors of a catalytic leader or teammate. While some human catalysts are strong in all of them, you can have a significant impact by mastering a core subset. We have organized them into four cornerstones, based on how they might be most effectively applied in new circumstances:

1. *Building Credibility*: Behaviors essential for developing trust, communicating effectively, and generating belief in what can be achieved.

2. *Creating Cohesion:* Behaviors that coalesce relationships and propel mission-oriented action.

3. *Generating Momentum*: Behaviors that elevate and accelerate performance.

4. *Amplifying Impact*: Behaviors that promote excellence and encourage innovation.

Embedded in these 4 cornerstones are the 12 catalytic skills we have identified that elevate individual and team performance.

Skills

Building Credibility

Acts with Integrity and Inspires Trust
Lives authentically. Demonstrates ethical principles and values in a manner that promotes trust.

Communicates Clearly
Actively speaks and writes in clear concise messages; listens closely for understanding. Employs creative ways to convey ideas, concepts, and content that cross cultural, language, and educational boundaries.

Invigorates with Optimism
Energizes others with a confident, hope-filled outlook on the future. Conveys a can-do attitude.

Creating Cohesion

Connects Emotionally
Acknowledges the emotional signals of others and responds empathetically.

Develops Camaraderie
Establishes a positive rapport and fosters constructive interactions.

Puts the Team's Goals and the Organization's Mission before Personal Interests
Prioritizes team success and process over personal goals. Selfless; does what it takes to achieve results by focusing on overarching organizational objectives.

Generating Momentum

Energizes Others to Execute with the Mission in Mind
Ignites others to achieve organizational objectives.

Upgrades and Rejuvenates Skills and Knowledge
Seeks and acquires leading-edge knowledge and expertise. Curious about new developments and concepts and how to apply them.

Leads and Follows
Leads when best qualified to accelerate progress toward objectives. Partners with others or follows the leadership of others when their knowledge and expertise are well suited to the task. Demonstrates respect for the abilities of others.

Amplifying Impact

Pursues Excellence
Demonstrates extensive knowledge or competence. Advocates for the high-caliber performance of others.

Mentors and Coaches Others to Excel
Models exemplary behavior and supports the personal and professional development of others by providing constructive advice.

Proposes Imaginative Solutions
Presents creative, imaginative, and value-adding ideas for solving problems and achieving objectives.

CORNERSTONE 1

BUILDING CREDIBILITY

TRUST, INTEGRITY, AND CREDIBILITY: HALLMARKS OF A CATALYST

Who will rally with you or for you in the absence of trust? In the absence of trust who will rush to your side to help move the team forward?

How important is it for colleagues and teammates to believe in your integrity, to have confidence in your motivations, and to have a conviction that you're shooting straight with them and will stand behind your words?

The key question is, what can truly be accomplished with others without personal credibility? Think of a person you would follow to the ends of the Earth. He or she is probably someone you trust, believe in, and whom you see as fully committed to achieving common goals and objectives. They invigorate those around them. *Credibility is the grease for catalytic action.* When it exists in large doses, the gears of teamwork can spin smoother and faster. Being that lubricant, and being viewed by others as such, sets up the catalytic team engine to run at peak effectiveness. And it sparks reciprocity among team members, which builds greater trust and optimism, and further accelerates a team's progress.

Building Credibility is the first of the four cornerstones of the Catalyst Effect. It is the most basic building block and is a critical piece of being a catalytic leader. Leadership researchers and acclaimed authors, James M. Kouzes and Barry Z. Posner, have determined that "...credibility is the foundation of leadership..." (Kouzes & Posner, 2011, p. xvii). We would extend that beyond leadership to all relationships that work. The following three chapters explore the path for building credibility by focusing on three individual competences:

- Acts with Integrity and Inspires Trust.

- Communicates Clearly.

- Invigorates with Optimism.

Of the more than 80 interviews we conducted across the sectors of business, sports, and the arts, virtually everyone pointed to credibility as the foundation for being a positive catalytic influence.

1

ACTS WITH INTEGRITY AND INSPIRES TRUST

Definition: Lives authentically. Demonstrates ethical principles and values in a manner that promotes trust.

Counter Behaviors: Deceitful, dishonest, fails to meet commitments.

IT TAKES MORE THAN JUST SHOWING UP

Against great odds and most predictions, the Butler University men's basketball team played in two NCAA Final Four Championship games in 2010 (versus Duke) and 2011 (versus UConn). With an enrollment of about 4500 students, Butler was the smallest school to play for a national championship since the tournament expanded to 64 teams in 1985.

Ron Nored was a key — some would say *the* key to the team's success. He is not a household name in college basketball lore, but he was a *glue-guy*. Ron, a six-foot point guard, was not a stat-stuffing player but ultimately was pivotal to the team's success. He rarely scored the most points or grabbed the most rebounds, yet he typified the concept of the *no-stats all-star* who makes everyone better when he or she is on the floor.

In an interview with Kent Sterling, a CBS Sports host, Nored recalled the commitment of the team and the trust they established (Sterling, 2010). He spoke of getting up promptly at 5:30 am when the alarm went off, and by 6:30 sharp he was practicing hard with his teammates. He loved the sight of the historic Hinkle Fieldhouse and recalled how the combination of the gym's cool, fresh air and the sounds of bouncing basketballs were simply beautiful. He and his teammates were well beyond the mental challenge of getting out of bed, and to a person, each player was pumped up and ready to become a little bit better that day.

> When we meet someone new, we quickly answer two questions:
> 'Can I trust this person and can I respect this person?'
> — Amy Cuddy, Presence: Bringing Your Boldest Self
> to Your Biggest Challenges (2015)

Of course, each player showed up on time and ready to practice, but Nored's enthusiasm and influence stood out. He usually led by being the first player in the gym, making it a point to personally say something to each other player, chat with the coaches, and set the standard for early morning hustle. He served as a glue-guy on a high intensity team of highly skilled athletes. As a result, there was a trust among this group of young men and a commitment to practicing hard and giving of oneself to improve as individuals and as a team. The coaches were caring mentors, always there with a smile and a "great to see you!"

Through this reflection, *an important slice of what constitutes integrity and trust is revealed: reliability, demonstrated commitment, high performance ethic, and being present for others.* These factors exemplify a desire to produce and help others excel. Yet they are only part of the equation. They prove that one can be counted on. Still, there is an additional, equally important side of integrity and trust that the team exemplified. Let's take a look.

Brad Stevens, head coach of the Bulldogs during those tournament runs, shared his perspective with us as to why Ron was so critical to the team (personal communication, December 14, 2009). While Stevens mentioned that Ron had a respectable number of assists, something expected of players in Ron's position, and his ability to stifle opposing guards, he didn't spend much time talking about them. Instead, he emphasized that Ron brought authenticity and credibility to the team in everything he did whether it was in the locker room, on the practice court, in games, or in his school and personal life. Everyone knew they could trust Ron to do what he said he would do for the good of the team and his teammates. He was consistent in all that he said and what we all saw him do. Beyond that, though, Nored embodied a set of core beliefs that reflected the philosophy of The Butler Way, crafted by legendary coach Tony Hinkle in the 1920s (Hein, n.d.):

1. Humility: Those who humble themselves will be exalted.

2. Passion: Do not be lukewarm; commit to excellence.

3. Unity: Do not divide our house; team first.

4. Servanthood: Make teammates better; lead by giving.

5. Thankfulness: Learn from every circumstance.

> *People form opinions about the integrity of their teammates, cowor-kers, and friends based on observable patterns of behavior.*

Nored brought Hinkle's five core principles to life in his day-to-day actions on the court as well as in the classroom by

- Being humble. Those who were in class with Ron would never suspect that he was a star player. He worked diligently alongside every other student and expected no special treatment.

- Expressing his commitment to excellence. He showed up early, stayed late, watched game film, and did all the little things elite, committed players do on and off the court.

- Putting team first. His body language and encouraging words showed he put the team ahead of himself. If there was conflict in the locker room, he helped end it in a manner that was best for the team, not for certain individuals.

- Displaying little ego. He exuded an enthusiasm that was directed toward helping others, whether with defensive positioning, shooting technique, or homework. He was the epitome of Coach Stevens' widely quoted comment: "We're building a culture of accountability, trust, and togetherness. Entitlement will not be tolerated."

- Exhibiting incredible curiosity. He was dedicated to studying the opposing players' habits and developing offensive and defensive strategies.

Consistently applying positive values leads to trust, and trust leads to credibility. Being true to one's values, especially in high pressure and challenging situations, when it would be easier or more convenient to be expedient or self-focused, is the mark of character. If those around you know what you stand for and that you will consistently adhere to those values, they will trust that you will act accordingly. Situational ethics or the inconsistent application of values rarely engenders respect.

WHAT IS INTEGRITY? WHAT IS TRUST? WHY ARE THEY SO IMPORTANT?

How can others tell if you have integrity? From an impact standpoint, all that matters is what others see and believe about you, not what you may feel or think about yourself. People form opinions about the integrity of their teammates, coworkers, and friends based on observable patterns of behavior: honesty in how they portray their own work and describe circumstances, truthfulness in owning up to mistakes or lapses in judgment, application of ethical principles in decision-making and handling of routine and difficult situations, and moral constancy. It is through these actions that integrity, an intangible, becomes visible and evident to others. Evidence of integrity affects how people react to you.

How can others tell if they can trust you? Integrity is an integral part of trust. Trust, however, encompasses a broader set of characteristics. Others learn to trust you when they see that your stated intentions match your actions and that you will deliver on what you promise. Trust grows stronger when you consistently deliver on those commitments and behave ethically. *When others trust you, they know you will do what's right and be a reliable team member.* Trust also creates a feeling of emotional safety that leads others to confide and work in partnership with you, knowing their disclosures and vulnerabilities will not be exploited. It creates a feeling that you are on the same team in actuality and in personal spirit.

People may need time to assess your integrity, trustworthiness, and overall character once they meet you. Conclusions are usually reached over the course of multiple experiences, especially in the absence of contrary evidence, such as obvious lies, shading of the truth, cheating, and other unethical behavior. While the performance and teamwork benefits of high integrity may roll out slowly, the adverse consequences of unethical behavior are immediate:

- Disbelief in what you stand for and your dedication to supporting team objectives.

- Loss of credibility.

- Diminished cooperation, collaboration, and communication.

- Guardedness and avoidance.

- Others watching their backs, feeling suspicious, fearing betrayal.

When you behave unethically you may also find yourself defending against blame, fending off accusations, or being caught in a web of deceit. These inhibiting behaviors negatively impact performance. Energy and focus is diverted from accomplishing team goals to protecting personal interests.

High integrity and trust have the opposite impact: greater belief in who you are, higher credibility, greater collaboration and communication, openness, partnership, and uninhibited pursuit of common goals. These fuel catalytic performance.

> *Applied values drive how you resolve problems, settle ethical dilemmas, develop and nurture relationships, and follow through on your intentions.*

LIVE YOUR VALUES CONSISTENTLY

Ron Nored's values and skills did not single-handedly propel the Butler Bulldogs to back-to-back NCAA Championship finals — that was achieved by the entire team. Yet he was a catalyst and the lubricant that helped drive the Bulldogs' success against much higher-ranked teams from far larger schools. These were teams well stocked with "blue-chip" players that Butler, as a small school with fewer athletic resources, had greater difficulty attracting. Nored promoted Butler's values and the idea that, to make the team greater than the sum of its parts, they had to trust each other to perform and help each other play their best. The same holds true in all other fields of endeavor whether that be in business, the arts, philanthropic organizations, or others.

Nored demonstrated that values are only truly conveyed — and are only believed and realized — through action. Integrity, authenticity, and trust cannot be proclaimed. They become real through sustained patterns of behavior — by consistently living those values.

VALUES: THE CORE OF WHO YOU ARE

Values define the nucleus of your being. They are your *how's*. Applied values drive how you resolve problems, settle ethical dilemmas, develop and nurture relationships, and follow through on your intentions.

Beyond being true to oneself and fostering trust, consistent observable demonstration of one's values makes you more approachable. Others are more likely to listen to your advice as problems or dilemmas arise. Trust engenders robust exchanges of useful information and expertise. For catalysts, this is key to their influence and ability to help others perform at higher levels.

The literature describes three dimensions of trust within a team that are important to knowledge creation and sharing: ability ("I trust that you know what you are talking about"), benevolence ("I trust that you care about my well-being and goals"), and integrity ("I trust that I can take you at your word") (Mayer, Davis, & Schoorman, 1995).

Rob Cross, a professor at the University of Virginia, and his team explain that "benevolence-based trust" opens the door for others to "query a colleague in depth without fear of damage to self-esteem or reputation." (Abrams, Cross, Lesser, & Levin, 2003) When this aspect is coupled with a perception of ability in the other person (or high competence), confidence in that individual grows further. The two in combination lay the groundwork for catalysts to have a profound impact on others' and team performance overall.

So, this insight begs the question — are your core values apparent in your daily interactions and in how you work? Do they demonstrate integrity and engender trust? What are they?

IDENTIFYING AND DEMONSTRATING YOUR VALUES

What are your five or six core personal values? Take stock of them and refer to them as reminders of the person you most want to be. Use them as guides when you are uncertain how to make a decision and let them guide your decision-making — which in turn keeps you true to yourself or *authentic*. Like Brad Stevens, we believe that your values reflect the core of your integrity. Through them, others will know what to expect of you.

If you are new to a team or organization, begin demonstrating your guiding values on your first day. It's much harder to build credibility from an eroded position than to establish it from the start of a relationship. If you do need to make up ground, start living your values consistently going forward. Eventually, you will offset contrary impressions if you are to be perceived as authentic.

RECHARGE YOUR TRUST BATTERY

We have operationalized a set of behaviors that demonstrate to others that you, a catalyst, are someone who lives, speaks, and acts authentically — and that a strong ethical footing supports this authenticity. Stating what you believe, stating what you will do, and then acting consistently with those statements leads people to trust you. A full "trust battery" as described by Shopify's Lütke energizes others (Bryant, 2016). It drains when you:

- Apply your values inconsistently.

- Fail to meet commitments.

- Behave in a way that creates suspicion about your motivations.

- Demonstrate any of the contrary behaviors mentioned earlier.

Remember that the fastest destroyer of trust and esprit de corps is suspicion of self-serving, ulterior motives.

Steven M.R. Covey in his business bestseller, *The Speed of Trust*, discusses the insidious nature of what he calls "counterfeit" trust behaviors (Covey & Merrill, 2008). These behaviors are perhaps worse than the opposite behaviors. Counterfeit behaviors are designed to create the impression of trust, but are manipulative; they erode teamwork, foment suspicion, damage relationships, and impair performance. Covey offers many examples of what these behaviors look like. A trust behavior would be speaking honestly and straightforwardly. The opposite behavior would be to lie or deceive. The counterfeit behavior would be actively manipulating the thoughts, feelings, or actions of another — indulging in double-talk, empty compliments, withholding information, or creating false impressions. If one is trustworthy, that person admits to making a mistake and trying to remedy it. Counterfeit behaviors often serve to cover up mistakes and blame others.

Occasionally, all of us have trust and integrity lapses and may find ourselves displaying *counterfeit* or *opposite* trust behaviors. The key to restoring trust, to getting things back on track, is to acknowledge our lapses and make things right. The courage to do that garners respect and helps recharge our trust batteries. Trust batteries can only be recharged or replenished through tangible action, ethical decisions, acknowledging and correcting mistakes, and genuine problem-solving — in routine and exceptional situations.

Values represent what you stand for. When you don't follow through, you diminish your posture — your character and status — in both your own eyes and the eyes of others.

INTEGRITY AND TRUST

Catalytic performance depends on trust, and integrity is one of its primary attributes. The trust literature is consistent in its findings that people charge forward when they know they can rely on each other and understand what to expect — and believe that others will do what is right. Agreements can be sealed with a handshake; a nod of assent can suffice for detailed explanations, contracts, or negotiations; checks and balances become less necessary. All of those consume time. High trust among people and within teams pays off; results are achieved faster with less wear and tear. Additionally, high-trust relationships, both within and between organizations, lead to far better performance than when burdened with the suspicion and doubts that accompany low trust (Barney & Hansen, 1994).

> *Whoever is careless with the truth in small matters, cannot be trusted with important matters.*
> —Albert Einstein quoted in Albert Einstein,
> Historical and Cultural Perspectives (1997)

In *Great Places to Work: The Business Case of a High-Trust Culture* (2016), multiple examples show that firms with high-trust environments are more successful in recruiting and retaining talent. Although all of these positive outcomes occur at the organizational level, trust must start with individuals. It can start with a single catalyst acting authentically and with integrity. It can start with you!

Failure to act with integrity and failing to kindle and sustain trust may lead your teammates and others in the organization to question virtually everything about you. Your request to work remotely, to be put in charge of a project, to be given significant responsibility, or to garner access to sensitive information may all be questioned. Your ability to influence others will be lower and your opportunities to develop will diminish.

CONCLUSION

Our field research shows that integrity and trust are fundamental *currencies of entry* or what an individual needs to invest to be an integral part of a team. Without demonstration of these characteristics through action, so they are visible to others, team members will have difficulty becoming influential catalysts. Virtually everyone we interviewed stressed that the concepts of trust and integrity arise from a strong, positive set of personal values that underlie all other actions a team member takes. If they are missing, other skills and strengths mean little over the long run.

One earns another's trust not just by delivering brilliant ideas, but by keeping small, individual commitments. When the deadline for a report is the end of the week, meet or beat it. When the team needs you to support a project that is not necessarily your job, assist anyway. Be relentless in keeping your commitments and in valuing the team and your teammates.

Take a moment to reflect on your own behavior, do you:

- Live your values consistently?

- Align intentions with the greater good?

- Keep personal ego and ambition in check?

- Keep commitments and promises?

- Act and speak honestly?

- Take immediate action to repair lost trust and credibility?

2

COMMUNICATES CLEARLY

Definition: Actively speaks and writes in clear concise messages; listens closely for understanding. Employs creative ways to convey ideas, concepts, and content that cross cultural, language, and educational boundaries. Breaks through communication barriers to achieve results.

Counter Behaviors: Communicates little or ambiguously; ignores suggestions and input of others.

COMMUNICATING ACROSS BOUNDARIES

When Yo-Yo Ma asked Sandeep Das, a member of the Silk Road Ensemble and one of the best tabla musicians in the world, to write an original piece for the Ensemble, Yo-Yo Ma did not realize this was a far more complex request than he originally thought (personal communication, 2016).

In 1998, Yo-Yo Ma formed the group as a collaboration of world-class artists from different musical backgrounds who played instruments unique to their countries. Sandeep joined the Silk Road Ensemble in 2000 while living in India. After his wildly successful career as a musician, Yo-Yo Ma's passion was to build an ensemble that brought together the "music of the world." As he expressed in a film documentary, *The Music of Strangers* (Neville, 2015), he believed that the world did not need another excellent cello player, and questioned what more he could contribute from that time forward. This triggered his journey to create something unique in the music world that crossed styles, instruments, and most importantly, cultures. Hence, the Silk Road Ensemble. The ensemble is not a fixed group of musicians, but rather a critically acclaimed collective of nearly 60 musicians, composers, arrangers, visual artists, and storytellers primarily from Eurasian cultures. *The Music of Strangers* portrays the group and is a testament to the power of culture-transcending music.

Sandeep has been nominated for two Grammy Awards. In 2003, his recording *The Rain* was nominated in the World Music category. In 2009, a recording with the Silk Road Ensemble was nominated in the Classical Crossover section for the album *Off the Map*. As a cultural and educational entrepreneur, Sandeep founded Harmony and Universality through Music, an ensemble of world-class artists whose goal is to promote global understanding through musical performance and education.

Back to Yo-Yo Ma's request...

Of course, Sandeep created the piece Yo-Yo invited him to compose. However, it was complicated because Sandeep did not, and could not, produce sheet music or classic scores for other musicians since he had never been trained to write them. Therefore, he communicated his ideas for the music verbally, describing the *colors* he wished to create, the beat and pace of the music via his demonstrations, and he described the feelings that he wished to create in those who would eventually hear and experience the piece.

> *I've learned that people won't remember what you said, and people won't remember what you did, people will only remember how you made them feel.*
> — Maya Angelou quoted in Robin Amos Kahn, "It Doesn't Matter What You Say: Lessons Learned from Maya Angelou and Pema Chodron," *Huffington Post*, (March 25, 2014)

Similarly, Sandeep was once asked to play a musical piece with a score. He demurred that he did not read music from a traditional score. He proposed that he simply listen to it once and that he would be able to play his part. The piece was 28 minutes long! The standard communication vehicle of written sheet music we usually associate with professional musicians, especially classical, was not the way he thought about playing or learning music. The score communicates primarily *what* is to be played, but not necessarily *how* it is to be interpreted. Even this alternative communication mode among strangers was effective because the musicians possessed a strong desire to connect with each other and understand how they could create the beautiful musical experience that others will appreciate and enjoy that Sandeep envisioned.

This Silk Road example underscores the idea that communication occurs in many different forms: verbal, nonverbal, auditory, visual, tactile, and the use of imagery that others can understand and interpret.

In Sandeep's situation, his primary communication mode was through a combination of auditory techniques and verbal imagery. The Silk Road Ensemble listens to each other intently and deeply to create a sound and experience that is unique every time they play. This catalytic approach to communication has helped them win four Grammy Awards, produce six albums and multiple singles to date, and consistently play to sold-out audiences all over the world.

THE FUNDAMENTALS OF EFFECTIVE COMMUNICATION

Communication among professional musicians in an international ensemble has unique characteristics. While music is a common denominator, their messaging must cross cultural boundaries. The musicians of the Silk Road Ensemble employ fundamental communication skills that each of us can develop and apply in challenging and routine circumstances. They are a prerequisite to having a catalytic influence.

Successful communication entails transmitting content and concepts from one mind into another's thought process. The transmission must be in a form that the sender can use effectively and that receivers can comprehend.

We all communicate in different ways — through our words, gestures, facial expressions, imagery, humor, other creative means, and even silence. How we communicate is far less important than the clarity of our messages. The only way we know if we've communicated clearly is through feedback from receivers. Only when they verify it verbally or confirm through their actions can we know for certain that they understood.

Misunderstandings often result in wasted effort. Statements or questions may be subject to varying interpretations. That's why verifying understanding is crucial to catalytic performance — at least until the team's shorthand and signals are well established. Verifying for understanding is a two-way process: verifying that others have understood you (through questions that elicit explanations or examples) and verifying that you have understood the other person (sometimes called active listening). We'll examine both of these techniques as well as several others later in this chapter.

Organizations and teams rely on effective communication to adapt quickly to challenging situations, respond adeptly to challenges, and react effectively to urgent conditions, whether within or across cultures, functions, and interest groups.

In most organizations, people in different departments have a lingo specific to their discipline — whether in finance, performance arts, information technology, public relations, engineering, research and development, or athletics. However, this is not necessarily true when communicating across cultures. Even gestures well understood in one culture may convey something entirely different in another. The same words or phrases may have different meanings or be seen in different contexts depending on where one sits.

While in China on business, one of our authors had to explain complex information to people who spoke little English, and he knew all of five words of Mandarin. Even with an interpreter, he wasn't sure from the nods, facial expressions, and short statements of agreement if his messages had been understood. What he soon realized, from the blank stares, was that people in that culture were extremely reluctant to ask questions or to indicate that they had not comprehended something. They were afraid to be wrong or embarrassed in front of colleagues and sometimes implied they understood when they really did not. He discovered that questions like, "Was that clear?" or "Did you understand?" resulted mostly in nods of assent and were little confirmation that the concepts had actually been grasped. His solution was to seek examples. The accuracy of the examples revealed whether he had been understood. When the examples missed the mark, he could assess where and how he had been misunderstood, then add clarity and offer additional examples of his own, while maintaining the self-esteem of each respondent. When he asked for subsequent examples, only when they captured the essence of the concepts was he sure his message had been conveyed. His success depended on making the exchange safe and checking for understanding in ways that fit the culture.

How often have you been in conversations in which someone kept saying what not to do — perhaps something like, "Don't do it the old way" or "Don't make that mistake again." Beyond being negative messages, these statements communicate nothing about what to do. For example, if you tell a child "Don't spill your milk," he or she is likely worried about making a mess. If you tell the child "Keep your elbows away from the table," you have offered a suggestion that is incompatible with milk spilling. It's positive behavioral guidance that creates precision, direction, and allows teams and organizations to act in a unified and aligned manner.

An old expression that contains enormous truth is "Actions speak louder than words." Nothing communicates more about your character, values, and what you truly intend than your own behavior. We identify role models by their behavior more than their speech. Nothing strengthens your credibility more than the alignment of your actions with your words. Actions, both as forms of communication and as outcome drivers, fuel catalytic teamwork.

Catalytic leaders and team members demonstrate a solid base of communication skills.

Nonverbal Communication

Body language, eye contact, hand gestures, and tone all color messages you are trying to convey. A relaxed, open stance (leaning forward with interest, arms open) and a friendly demeanor make one approachable and encourage others to communicate openly with you. Looking people in the eye in a comfortable way shows you are focused on them and what they have to say.

Active and Reflective Listening

Active listeners focus closely on what others are saying. They seek to understand both explicit and underlying messages and remember the content. Reflective listening entails rephrasing what the speaker was understood to say — as a way of clarifying and confirming that you interpreted it correctly ("So, what you're saying is..."). Listening skills, like all skills, improve with practice. Avoid thinking about other matters, or what you want to say, when others are talking. Active and reflective listening enables you to better understand what the other person is intending to say and respond appropriately — an essential skill for catalysts in both routine and complex conversations.

Asking Open-Ended and Thought-Provoking Questions

Great questions stimulate deeper thinking and help identify issues and solutions that may not be readily apparent. Engaging, open-ended questions — questions that stretch one's thinking — usually begin with what, how, why, or if:

- What would an ideal solution look like?

- What are the most important factors for accomplishing your goal?

- How can we check our assumptions?

- Why do you think customers reacted as they did?

- If our competitors did _____, what are our options?

- If we had a crisis because of _____, how could we address it?

Other information-generating inquires might begin with phrases such as:

- Walk me through...

- Tell me about...

- Describe....

- Give us an idea of how...

These types of queries open up communication and encourage discussions that clarify situations, uncover or analyze problems, identify opportunities, assess risks, and develop solutions — all of which contribute to catalytic performance. They take conversations to more productive levels, whether sorting through a decision process, developing innovative solutions, or striving to understand why there is disagreement.

Open-Mindedness

Asking questions and listening fully — without interrupting — to another person's point of view, rather than simply pushing your ideas, demonstrates a willingness to understand and consider carefully what he or she has to say — even when you disagree. It conveys the desire to have an honest, productive dialogue and an interest in uncovering common ground, which may be the basis for collaborative problem-solving, partnership, and joint action.

Communication Objectives

Develop communication goals based on your understanding of your audiences. Plan where you would like to take them and how. Most communications are intended to persuade either directly or subtly.

Know what you want to achieve. Decide what to emphasize. Identify the top three points you want your listeners to grasp and remember. Clear points made concisely and vividly are more powerful than long-winded explanations. A concluding call to action drives the purpose and importance of communications home. Articulate what you see as the next steps.

Listener or Audience Assumptions

Structure or organize communications based on your best assessment of the listeners' knowledge base, objectives, and predispositions. Most communication is intended to be persuasive. With that in mind, begin communicating with a clear understanding of your audience. The purpose is to cultivate the audience's understanding and to create alignment.

Storytelling

People remember colorful stories that make a point more than details and abstract concepts. You can bring your communications to life and have greater impact when you couple your content with stories that illustrate the points. Listeners are more likely to remember your message by recalling the stories that convey it.

Feedback

Giving feedback is a key catalytic skill. The best and most credible feedback is specific and actionable. Phrases like "good job," "way to go," "you can do better," and "that wasn't great" don't provide the specificity for someone to truly know what it was they did that worked and how to improve. Behavioral and pinpointed feedback is more valuable to the receivers. They will be less defensive and find it more helpful. Specific, behavioral feedback should include information about the:

- Circumstances.
- Objectives that were to be accomplished.

- Behaviors demonstrated/actions taken.

- Impact of the actions.

Content Value versus Volume

Effective communication is not determined by volume. It's the value and utility of the information that matters, especially inside a team or work group. In an article titled "Managing Collaboration at the Point of Execution," Rob Cross, a professor at the University of Virginia, in conjunction with several business colleagues explains that traditional team advice focuses on building commitment to a goal. In general, the tendency is to believe that more communication is better — but there is rarely any focus on the quality of the information or knowledge moving in the team (Cross, Ehrlich, Dawson, & Helferich, 2008).

Catalysts focus on the key points, the essential elements for decision-making, setting direction, boosting collaboration, and driving forward. In doing so, they break gridlocks that perpetuate conflict and decision paralysis — which consume unnecessary time and energy. Cross and his associates point out that the key to effectiveness is not the number or length of discussions but the number of productive, value-laden interactions — and decreasing or shortening those that go nowhere.

Sandeep's experience in the opening story illustrates what happens when a team and its members strive to understand each other and coalesce to produce exemplary work. They overcome barriers and focus on the objectives and tasks. This next story is in stark contrast, demonstrating how the inability to persuade and the unwillingness to listen can have tragic results.

THE CHALLENGER COMMUNICATION DISASTER

A communication breakdown killed seven astronauts. Rarely do communication failures have such catastrophic consequences, as they did for the Challenger space shuttle crew in 1986, but they almost always negatively affect teamwork, efficiency, work effectiveness, and frequently result in significant wastes of time, effort, and money.

The messaging and listening issues leading up to the Challenger disaster offers a compelling case in point. Engineers spent hours trying to convince managers that O-ring seals, which "prevent hot combustion gasses from escaping from the inside of the motor" (*The Engineer*, 2006), were at risk of failure due to wear-and-tear deterioration, and that the problem was especially acute when the launch temperature was under 53 degrees Fahrenheit. On January 28, 1986, the temperature at the Florida launch site was more than 30 degrees colder. Challenger exploded 73 seconds after lifting off on its tenth mission.

OVERCOMING COMMUNICATION BARRIERS

Why weren't the engineers' warnings heeded? Explanations vary but chief among them are skepticism, conflicting and incomplete data, arrogance, "groupthink," and pressure to launch. Even though the engineers' warnings were ominous, their concerns were not sent up the chain of command. Key decision makers were kept in the dark.

What can we learn from this episode? First, to recognize the ingredients inherent in it are part and parcel of many organizations, large and small. Catalytic performance depends on overcoming these issues. Each contributor is responsible for communicating clearly and ensuring messages from others are well understood.

Tuning out messages you don't want to hear squanders opportunities for improvement. It sacrifices the pursuit of solutions or more effective strategies. As with Challenger, it could also result in a preventable disaster.

Overcoming Skepticism and Objections

It begins with credibility and trust, which is the thrust of this catalytic cornerstone. The engineers at NASA had high technical credibility and presented data based on theoretical projections, yet somehow that was insufficient. Getting beyond the receiver's contention that "this consequence has never happened before, so why should we believe it will happen now?" is difficult, but not impossible. One key is to ask thought-inducing questions to engage listeners, to get them to think and examine issues more deeply, including implications. To address objections, ask additional questions to elicit their summary of what they understood, and to clarify as necessary.

The responsibility for clear communication lies with both sender and receiver.

> *The most important thing in communication is hearing what isn't said.*
>
> — Peter Drucker

Addressing Conflicting and Incomplete Data

Rarely is all conceivably relevant information available for making timely decisions. There are almost always things we don't know, and to acquire the information may push out the timeframe to unacceptable points or beyond when actually needed — whether that's a launch date, game time, or a project deadline. The same holds true when data or interpretations of data conflict with one another, making the path forward unclear. So what do you do? Resolve to make the best possible decision, having weighed the risks, with the information you have at the time — knowing the possibility for error and assuming accountability for potential repercussions if things go wrong. Catalytic leaders and team members crystalize the issues and the circumstances. They propose solutions or actions for breaking gridlock and moving forward with the best interests of the team and its objectives in mind.

Combatting Arrogance

Arrogance inhibits catalytic performance. It stymies the exploration of solutions that teams can wholeheartedly get behind.

Overpowering arrogance is among the toughest of communication challenges. Voss Graham, CEO of the InnerActive Consulting Group, explains that arrogance often stems from a "high need for structure" and inflexible thought processes (2008). Arrogant people are often locked into their own opinions, not open to others, and tend to "ignore new information or circumstances." (Graham, 2008) They don't just take pride in their work, which is a hallmark of good self-esteem, rather, they are *prideful*. They may also have an unjustifiable confidence that serves to mask insecurity about their own abilities or knowledge. They may act as if they are always right, know more than others, or as if they are the smartest person in the room.

For a communicator to prevail over the arrogance of a particular individual may require the skillful use of a variety of tools. That might be the only way to discover the most effective blend of interactive communications for breaking through it.

Overcoming another's arrogance requires specialized listening, questioning, and feedback techniques.

Listening

One approach is to focus on the content rather than the other person's attitude, arrogance, emotions, or body language when listening. In a composed manner, acknowledge and reply only to the substance; don't react to how the message is articulated but to the content of that message.

Questioning

Asking questions that get to the heart of the issue at hand is one way to actually make the conversation impactful and move it forward. Work to understand the person's thought process and examine the methods taken to arrive at his or her conclusion. Find out if the person is aware of data or information believed to be solid that was not part of his or her analysis. After reviewing this new information, explain how it gives you a different perspective on the matter and why. Then ask if changes in his or her assumptions or conclusions should be made. Above all else, stay nonconfrontational.

At this point, you have the opportunity to encapsulate your conclusions inside questions, for example: "How much do you know about how XYZ company handled a similar situation and what ultimately worked for them?" After hearing the reply, "I think there are some lessons they learned that might be helpful for us...such as..." "Do you see the parallels?" Take a stand and hold it, backing it with a fact-based comprehensive analysis. Don't pander.

Another approach is to mix purpose-oriented questions with relevant information to help them follow your logic, so they might arrive at your conclusion as if it were their own. This technique allows others to change their positions without losing face. Also, in the spirit of collaboration, ask if it would be helpful to explore the pros and cons of various options to reach the most well-thought-out decision. Suggest that it's often a good practice to look closely at three or more options before settling on one.

Feedback

By the time you arrive at the feedback phase, you will likely have a pretty good sense of the other person's approach and agenda. Keeping things moving forward in a feedback setting might be tricky, but you can make it productive by acknowledging what the other person says, asking clarifying questions, and respectfully summarizing your understanding. You also need to discern and acknowledge the other person's goals and objectives. This is a good way to find common ground and mutual goals.

Prevailing over Groupthink

In the 1970s, Irving Janis introduced the concept of *groupthink* (Janis, 1972). He studied this phenomenon mostly in political settings; however, whenever any group or team is convened, groupthink can overtake it. Groupthink is when the team makes faulty decisions because of group pressure. This pressure has two fundamental contributors: high levels of cohesiveness within the group and concurrence-seeking that leads individuals to agree with the consensus of the team rather than opposing it. These factors may result in poor or even critically faulty decision-making where agreement comes too quickly, when assumptions go unchallenged, and when closed-mindedness prevails. Closed-mindedness makes it impossible to single out problems in a decision because the group doesn't feel the need to do any further analysis or due diligence.

Although this concept dates back to the 1970s, it is still relevant today as noted in an updated version of Janis' ideas. The 2014 book titled *Crucial Decisions: Leadership in Policymaking and Crisis Management* applies his work to the business environment.

More recent studies of groupthink add the following indicators to the mix:

- Mindguards who are members of the group who push to retain the central group idea and omit information that may cause doubts about its viability.

- Apparent unanimity inside the group because dissenting views and objections are suppressed or discouraged and sometimes verbally punished.

- Illusion of invulnerability and overconfidence in the group's judgment.

- Illusion of morality, in which group members "lose sight of their personal moral principles" and allow the "overall morality of the group" to "override any individual sense of right and wrong."

- Biased opinions of the conclusions or findings of outside groups.

- Failure to establish contingency plans.

Breaking through group conformity is a formidable challenge that requires courageous, strong, and clear communications. It entails the ability to withstand powerful pushback and to speak convincingly. Catalytic leaders and team members achieve this through assertive and valiant communications that may include:

- Resisting rushes to judgment or quick unvetted decisions.

- Soliciting a wide range of opinions by stimulating debate and facilitating disagreement.

- Assuming the role of devil's advocate.

- Coaxing reluctant participants to speak up and present new ideas; then reinforcing their involvement.

- Advocating that three or more distinct options be objectively assessed prior to a final decision.

- Seeking and presenting best practices and novel solutions devised by other organizations.

Communicating effectively in the face of opposing opinions and pressure to conform to conventional thinking or strong group influencers is not easy. It requires strength of character and the courage of one's convictions.

CONCLUSION

Highly productive interactions are far more important than the amount of discussion. Openness, adaptability, and creativity in conveying and receiving messages and applying the content help propel catalytic performance. The absence of these factors inhibits it, as does intractable skepticism, arrogance, and groupthink. The Silk Road Ensemble's reaction to Sandeep Das illustrated the difference. Although the members have long histories of success and of doing things in a certain way, they did not close their minds to learning and communicating in new ways to accommodate Sandeep.

To succeed together as a diverse group, they had to be open to learning from each other and adapt. When Sandeep explained why he couldn't communicate the score he was proposing through classical sheet music, the other musicians embraced his unconventional way of transmitting and teaching the melodies that were only in his mind. Rather than resisting, they adapted. As a result, they created a sound that was unique to them and that was acclaimed worldwide.

Communicating complex information clearly requires a multifaceted skill set, in order to send and receive messages effectively and credibly, and achieve catalytic results.

Take a moment to reflect on your own behavior, do you:

- Speak honestly and authentically?

- Maintain eye contact when listening to others?

- Verify understanding both ways?

- Communicate clearly and concisely?

- Balance speaking and listening; ask powerful, high-value questions that will draw the speaker out?

- Seek and use examples?

- Shy away from tough conversations and communicating bad news?

- Open up conversations to opposing points of view in order to arrive at the best decision?

- Communicate methodically, knowing the goal of the conversation or meeting and keeping the various players' motivations and communication skills in mind?

- Align your actions with your words and let your character shine through?

3

INVIGORATES WITH OPTIMISM

Definition: Energizes others with a confident, hope-filled outlook on the future. Conveys a can-do attitude.

Counter behaviors: Saps others with negativity and pessimism; complains or gossips (often behind the backs of others).

OPTIMISM FUELS TEAM SUCCESS

The power of optimism in both what the people and the team can do are exemplified at a McDonald's restaurant near Indianapolis. One recently hired employee explained, "McDonald's gives people chances nobody else will. They expect us to succeed and let us know they think we can. That makes us better as individuals and as a crew." (personal communication, September 28, 2016)

For many new McDonald's hires, it is often the first time someone has shown confidence in them and the person they can become no matter what their work experience. The clear message is if you want to be part of a successful crew and are willing to do what it takes to help the team perform well, we want you to be part of our store — and we will help you excel and grow.

Knowing that not every employee can be proficient at everything from day one, the store finds initial roles in which each crewmember can experience success before being trained in more complex jobs. Their objective is to create *aces in their places*, which builds individual confidence and fosters higher crew performance.

So begins the process of Invigorating with Optimism. It underlies the culture and day-to-day work environment in this high-performing store. It is a propellant. It is contagious. It is ignited by the chance to learn a new job, to perform well, and to be reinforced by other crewmembers that have experienced similar successes. They learn to expect and encourage the best from one another, becoming catalysts to each other, by assisting whoever needs help to perform their job well. That's the essence of good teamwork.

At this particular location, we asked crewmembers who best typifies this energy — that ability to be a spark plug to the crew? Each person said, "That's Angie!" The crew's consensus: she enthusiastically raises the energy of the whole team! She responds to each of them with a positive word and a smile, which makes a difference in how their day goes, and how they do their work. The crew's optimism helps make this store one of the highest-performing locations in terms of guest satisfaction and employee engagement.

In quick-serve restaurants, speed and accuracy are critical. Think about your visits to fast-food restaurants. You immediately get a sense of how long the wait will be from seeing lines at the registers or the number of cars at the drive through. Beyond the "busy-ness" of the store, a key to speed and accuracy is the efficiency of the crew and its ability to coordinate effectively.

Optimism in each other fuels team success — and the confidence they can serve 300 meals in an hour when necessary — something most crewmembers thought was impossible when first hired. When they experience this first hand, when they are part of the action, they realize it is possible.

What does Invigorating with Optimism look like in practice? How do you know it when you see it? In the McDonald's crew, it includes forgiving errors and setting others up for success, both fellow teammates and the next shift. They serve as spark plugs to each other. "Can-do" is more than a slogan; it's a practice that permeates the crew, and it's coupled with smiles, positive attitudes, and a commitment to helping others grow. It's a quality that has enormous impact on the team and organization.

IMPACT OF OPTIMISM

How does optimism impact performance? Extensive research has shown how optimism generates purposeful energy, creative thinking, and a drive for results. Intel cofounder Robert Noyce said optimism is "an essential ingredient of innovation. How else can the individual welcome change over security, adventure over staying in safe places" (as cited in Gallo, 2012).

A study examining the impact of leadership optimism on information technology professionals, conducted by Margaret H. Greenberg and Dana Arakawa at the University of Pennsylvania, found that "positive leadership is correlated with employee engagement and performance," and demonstrates "the importance of optimism in the workplace." (Greenberg & Arakawa, 2006) The study reveals significant positive correlations between a leader's positive perspective and employee optimism.

Optimism propels performance, even in unfavorable circumstances.

Optimism is a key ingredient in entrepreneurial and business success. A driving force for starting a company is optimism in one's own abilities to generate a profitable business along with the ability to positively mobilize others in achieving results, starting essentially with an idea, some funding, and little more. A 2013 survey conducted for the Ewing Marion Kauffman Foundation by LegalZoom found that "91% of entrepreneurs were confident that their businesses would be more profitable in the next 12 months." (as cited in Campbell, 2014) Yet most did not expect the economy to improve in the following year — which, unlike their business, was something over which they had no control. Among the 91% who were confident in the future of their enterprise, 49% were very confident.

Optimism propels performance, even in unfavorable circumstances — whether that is a poor economy, stiff competition, setbacks, or poor publicity. Optimism has the power to galvanize — to catalyze — and be a force for turning performance around and rebuilding momentum. Optimism and a belief in what could be achieved helped drive some of the world's most successful companies through daunting circumstances, including Microsoft, Hyatt Hotels, FedEx, Revlon Cosmetics, and General Electric (Investopedia, n.d.). More recently, in the recession that began in the 2007–2008 timeframe, several highly successful companies were launched. Examples include the restaurant chain Smash Burger, the social media sensations Pinterest and Instagram, and online retailer Zappos. Optimism can cut through tough economic times.

Optimism has the power to galvanize — to catalyze — and be a
force for turning performance around and rebuilding momentum.

In the world of sports, leadership and teammate optimism in what can be accomplished helped move numerous teams from among the worst to the top in their leagues. Prominent examples include the 2013 Auburn Tigers (college football), the 2001 New England Patriots (pro football), the 2013 Boston Red Sox (pro baseball), the 1999 Indianapolis Colts (pro football), the 2005 Phoenix Suns (pro basketball), the 1991 Atlanta Braves (pro baseball), the 2007 Boston Celtics (pro basketball), and the 2016 Chicago Cubs (pro baseball).

OPTIMISM IN PRACTICE

Invigorating with Optimism extends the "power of positive thinking," popularized in Norman Vincent Peale's book of the same name (Peale, 2003). His focus is mostly on the self and is inwardly directed. Invigorating with Optimism as an aspect of the Catalyst Effect is outwardly directed and behaviorally visible. It's about demonstrating belief in others and what a team can achieve in a way that influences individual and team performance.

Invigorating with Optimism conveys a *can-do* spirit. We've all encountered people at the other end of the continuum — *can't-do* advocates. They are quick to cite reasons why something cannot be accomplished and why efforts to try are a waste of time and energy. If naysayers had prevailed, people would have never landed on the moon; the "bionic eye" named Argus II that allows the blind to see basic images would never have been invented; and you wouldn't have a smartphone in your pocket or bag. All of these, and much more, came about because optimists believed they were possible — which triggered high-energy, catalytic undertakings that brought them to fruition.

Central to Invigorating with Optimism is the strong and shared belief that a team or organization can rise to great heights, whether from great depths or the middle of the pack, and reinvent or differentiate itself with its own winning formula. Like the McDonald's crew, we've seen this phenomenon in other organizations.

Take Marvel Comics for example. Many great comic book stories have a darkest-hour moment: a point in the tale where all seems lost. The heroes are on their knees, the city is smoldering in ruins, and the villains are closing in for the kill. For Marvel, this story was very real: in the mid-1990s they were on the brink of bankruptcy and failure.

In the 1980s and early 1990s, while Marvel and the comics industry as a whole seemed in terrific health, Neil Gaiman, a highly successful comic book writer, argued that "the comic book market was an economic bubble — brought on by encouraging collectors to buy multiple editions and hoard them with the hope they would one day be worth a fortune." Gaiman predicted that this bubble was about to burst. He compared it to the Dutch tulip mania during the 17th century, a time when the price of tulip bulbs exploded due to high but unsustainable demand, and then fell precipitously as demand collapsed.

But like Kamala Kahn, a comic book super heroine, Marvel as a company possessed the optimism and the power to heal itself after a near-death experience.

To make a long story short, Marvel's small group of forward-thinking investors had a clear vision and charted a path for transforming the company. Their boldest decision was to become a player in the film industry. Avi Arad and Isaac Perlmutter brokered a deal to make an *X-Men* movie. Other blockbusters followed, including *Spider-Man*, *The Avengers*, and *Guardians of the Galaxy*.

These leaders brought to the team the optimism and passion necessary for others to believe in their vision, along with the wherewithal for acquiring the resources and financing to bring their vision to life.

For a company that was deep in debt less than 20 years ago, Marvel emerged from the jaws of defeat and in its darkest hour. Like the optimism and the ability to heal that Kamala Kahn brought to her character, this small team of catalysts invigorated the business and took it to new heights.

> *Authentic leadership is leading adaptively from your core, choosing who you're most inspired to be to serve the greatest good in this moment.*
>
> — Henna Inam, Wired for Authenticity: Seven Practices to Inspire, Adapt, and Lead (2015)

INVIGORATING WITH OPTIMISM IS APPLIED
PSYCHOLOGICAL CAPITAL

Why does optimism make such a difference?

A phenomenon called positive psychological capital (PsyCap) by organizational behavior scholars explains it. The lead researcher, Dr. Fred Luthans, a pioneer in the field of organizational behavior, along with several colleagues, has written extensively on the topic. Four core dimensions form the nucleus of PsyCap (Luthans, Youssef, & Avolio, 2007). All of these are learnable and collectively have a positive impact on performance. They include:

- Self-efficacy (confidence in one's ability to tackle challenging tasks and achieve desired objectives).

- Hope.

- Realistic optimism.

- Psychological resilience (the capacity to adapt successfully to unfavorable changes in circumstances and rebound from setbacks or failures).

These are also essential elements for Invigorating with Optimism. Their confluence elevates individual and team performance as revealed in subsequent research by Luthans and others, published in *Human Resources Development Quarterly* (Avey, Reichard, Luthans, & Mhatre, 2011; Luthans, Avey, Avolio, & Peterson, 2010). The body of this and other research, including our own, shows that people and teams that apply PsyCap and Invigorate with Optimism:

- Perform at higher levels — and sustain those levels.

- Energize others (in essence, they have a catalytic impact).

- Enjoy their jobs more.

- Have greater organizational commitment.

- Develop multiple options for meeting challenges and problem solving.

- Maintain positive can-do outlooks.

- Spring back constructively from setbacks.

- Support organizational change and show flexibility in adapting to it (Avey, Luthans, & Wernsing, 2008).

For leaders, the big question is how to make PsyCap and Invigorate with Optimism concepts actionable. We have identified the how-to practices and mapped the links between them, the four PsyCap benefits, and the organizational outcomes. They are delineated in the table below. The left-hand column lists catalytic practices, the center column shows the link between those practices and individual PsyCap benefits, and the right-hand column identifies the big-picture organizational impact.

THE IMPACT OF PESSIMISM

If optimism is a catalytic influence, what is the damage caused by pessimism or negativity? A post on "Emotional Management: The Impact of Negativity on Team Performance," by Australian business coach David Guest (2017) identifies several adverse effects. Pessimism:

- Reduces cooperation among team members.

- Weakens team unity.

- Breeds interpersonal conflict.

- Stymies forward progress.

- Dampens team morale.

- Erodes team work ethic.

Guest (2017) makes the point that "despite raging emotions or conflicts" an organization can emerge and develop a positive and effective culture.

A conscientious strategy to cultivate such a culture, understanding that emotions and attitudes influence how a person performs, is key. By changing people's outlook, you can transform the culture — whether you are a manager, team leader, or team member. The results may appear in many forms. For Shane Battier, the NBA basketball player, the evidence showed up on the scoreboard and in his teammates' stats. He also improved team cultures and camaraderie. In business, it may be reflected in time to market, quality improvement, cross-functional cooperation, and

How Invigorating with Optimism Connects to Organizational Impact

Catalytic Practices	PsyCap Benefits	Potential Organizational Impact
• Model successful behavior.		
• Demonstrate accountability.		
• Hold others accountable.		
• Learn task and goal-oriented material.	Self-Efficacy/Confidence	
• Apply strengths and tap the strengths of others.		
• Energize and refresh efforts.		
• Take moderate risks.		
• Define what success looks like.		
• Envision possibilities. Focus on realizing them.		
• Broadcast your optimism even during setbacks.		Heightened impact/ sustainable performance
• Challenge naysayers; focus on possibilities.		
• Set achievable goals for self and with your team.	Hope	
• Aspire and chart a clear path to success.		
• Anticipate obstacles and plan how they will be overcome, including possible contingency plans.		
• Expect unexpected challenges and develop a process for handling them to help stay on track.		

Realistic Optimism

- Believe in what you and your team can do.
- Develop and encourage positive expectancy.
- Develop/promote a culture of trust.
- Empower others with the belief that they can rise to the occasion.
- Motivate and coach with a "can-do" attitude — that combined, coordinated effort can produce extraordinary results.
- Focus on the sky, not the sludge.

Psychological Resilience

- Think fluidly and flexibly in response to challenges.
- Celebrate progress; reinforce effort and results.
- Build capacity for success and handling setbacks.
- Identify multiple paths to success and around barriers.
- See setbacks as occasions to find better ways.
- Focus energy and activity continually on goals.
- Stay passionate and purpose-oriented.
- Seek help, coaching, new perspectives, and best practices if you feel stuck or in a rut.
- Make fun part of the process.

employee engagement and loyalty, as well as on various effectiveness and efficiency measures.

HOW THE McDONALD'S CREW EXEMPLIFIES INVIGORATING WITH OPTIMISM

We began our discussion of Invigorating with Optimism with a story about a high-performing McDonald's crew. The practices for Invigorating with Optimism permeate its culture and the crew's mindset. The onboarding process begins with instilling a can-do spirit. As one employee said, "They expect us to succeed and let us know they think we can." (personal communication, September 28, 2016) This positive expectancy carries through to how the crews are led and the belief they express in each other and their team.

> *Catalysts strive to win over both hearts and minds to motivate and propel progress.*

Self-efficacy and confidence are developed through the modeling of effective performance and perpetuation of this can-do ethic. It begins by matching initial jobs to individual strengths to build confidence through early wins — "aces in their places" as they call the practice. (personal communication, September 28, 2016) Managers, crew leaders, and peers reinforce task and job effectiveness. As a result, self-confidence grows, becomes internalized, and these once new hires become performance models and mentors for others — and the cycle begins anew.

Hope is grown as crewmembers see new possibilities for themselves and their team. As part of a flourishing enterprise, they begin to envision future paths and opportunities that had not been apparent before — building on tangible successes. Setting goals and developing new aspirations is encouraged, enabling employees and the crew as a whole to envision more and reach higher.

Psychological resilience in a fast-food restaurant is required when things don't go as planned or how they normally would. Equipment may malfunction; deliveries may be delayed; accidents may have a negative impact on people and process; a normally slow period may become very busy — requiring a small crew to respond rapidly, efficiently, and effectively. Preparation and training for these unexpected events builds the resilience and the mindset to mobilize effectively. Each individual must think and act flexibly, perhaps taking on additional responsibilities seamlessly.

Whether a business, organization, or team is large or small, a foundation for success is established when individuals and groups Invigorate with Optimism. We've seen it repeatedly in a wide range of organizations — from the McDonald's restaurant to Marvel Comics to sports teams, and many others.

CONCLUSION

In a work environment, catalysts energetically promote the free flow of ideas to accelerate progress, heighten performance, and develop solutions. They encourage others to build on ideas and reinforce the practice. They invigorate and revitalize. They put ideas and solutions in motion with an air of optimism or enthusiasm.

In the next chapter, we discuss the importance of connecting emotionally. Invigorating with Optimism entails making positive emotional bridges coupled with an affirmative intellectual spirit in which concepts and plans are constructively and vibrantly explored. Catalysts strive to win over both hearts and minds to motivate and propel progress.

Take a moment to reflect on your own behavior, do you:

- Broadcast your own optimism and convey it even during setbacks?

- Empower others with the belief that they can rise to the occasion?

- Motivate your team with a can-do attitude — that combined, coordinated effort can produce extraordinary results?

- Promote the four elements of PsyCap: self-confidence, hope, optimism, and resilience?

- Challenge naysayers? Ask them to focus on the possible. Can't-do mindsets lead nowhere.

- Encourage others with tips for improving performance and belief in their ability to succeed?

- Find the tasks best suited for a person's existing strengths? Create initial success by identifying the best places for creating new aces?

- Spread the optimistic philosophy? Make it part of the culture in which everyone embraces it?

CORNERSTONE 2

CREATING COHESION

TOP TEAM PERFORMANCE REQUIRES COHESION

Teams perform at the highest level when they are cohesive. A unified force drives performance more powerfully than a divided one. Catalysts strengthen team unity and help overcome divisiveness. They unite team members for a common cause.

Common purpose is the bedrock of cohesiveness.

Cohesiveness is the extent to which team members stick together and remain united in the pursuit of a common goal (Molnau, 2017). You see true cohesion when individuals put the team's goals ahead of personal interests. As Linda Hill and Kent Lineback write in the *Harvard Business Review*, "A clear and compelling purpose is the glue that binds together a group of individuals. It is the foundation on which the collective 'we' of a real team is built." (2011) *Common purpose is the bedrock of cohesiveness.*

Highly cohesive teams concentrate on problem-solving, reaching objectives, and improving processes. Team members demonstrate a respect for each other and a commitment to supporting team decisions and strategies. They embrace accountability for themselves and emphasize it for all on the team and the team as a whole. The benefits include higher morale, improved communication, a congenial team environment, loyalty, and greater engagement in team decision-making (Daft & Marcic, 2009).

WHAT IS THE PURPOSE OF A TEAM AND WHAT MAKES IT COHESIVE?

Teams exist in all walks of life and in every type of work. The one thing all teams have in common is a purpose that defines their reason for existing. Sports teams exist to win games and championships. Business teams exist to accomplish goals for fulfilling the organization's mission. In government, teams exist to serve the public. In education, teams exist to promote learning. Community service teams exist to improve local conditions. Artistic teams exist to entertain or enlighten. The purpose of teams is to fulfill a mission more effectively than individuals can when working alone.

Catalysts strengthen the bonds between interdependent roles to create a cohesive whole dedicated to the group's purpose. Productive collaboration among both generalists and specialists drives team success and the team's ability to perform at a high level. Cohesion accelerates progress.

Jim Thorne, an experienced human resources leader and consultant whom we interviewed, insightfully observed that "catalysts have relatively low ego needs and a high passion to contribute." (personal communication, January 21, 2015) Their contributions frequently focus on the greater good for the team and creating a sense of togetherness.

Social scientists have invested heavily in research on team dynamics and group cohesion. Attraction to the group and its members is a contributing factor as is group pride (Hogg, 1992). The bottom line is that group cohesion evolves from a deep sense of "we-ness." (Bollen & Hoyle, 1990) In practice, cohesion comes from group members' commitment to work together to complete their shared tasks and accomplish collective goals. These bonds of unity reflect group cohesion (Guzzo & Salas, 1995).

BUILD ON CREDIBILITY TO CREATE COHESION

The second catalytic cornerstone, Creating Cohesion, flows naturally from the establishment of credibility — our first catalytic cornerstone. Without credibility, it's nearly impossible to develop team cohesion. The process requires leadership and influence. Others follow the lead of those who are trusted — who have shown themselves to have integrity, an optimistic outlook, and the right motivations. Creating team or group cohesion requires strong human connections. These relationships are developed through application of the three competencies encompassed in this cornerstone:

- Connects Emotionally.

- Develops Camaraderie.

- Puts the Team's Goals and the Organizational Mission before Personal Interests.

4

CONNECTS EMOTIONALLY

Definition: Acknowledges the emotional signals of others and responds empathetically.

Counter Behaviors: Aloof from others, ignores what others are feeling or criticizes their emotions; indifferent.

EMPATHY IN ACTION

The news of our company being acquired was not shocking. We knew our parent corporation had been considering divestiture of the agricultural business for several years. But when it finally occurred, it triggered a long list of questions relating to my career, my future, and my colleagues' futures — and whether we would feel any connection to the new organization and if the new management team would value us.

Would I be offered an opportunity with the new company? If so, in what role and at what level?

I was living and working in France, so would a new role be back home or still overseas? My spouse had a career as well. Would the new company assist him in finding a job? My daughter loved her school. Would we find a wonderful one for her in a new location?

It was with many of these questions and concerns in mind that I met with the CEO of the new parent company. Without my saying a word after we greeted each other, he seemed to sense my worries, as if he had once been in my place. Through his genial and reassuring manner, he put me at ease in moments. His easy smile, warm eye contact, and casual way of speaking made an immediate impression. He came across as genuine and as someone *truly interested in who I am as a person and a professional. His manner and his thoughtful questions instilled trust and showed a desire to see the situation through my eyes. In my gut, I felt a connection and that this was a first step toward developing a working relationship based on mutual respect and honesty.*

He devoted an extended period of time to fully answer my questions (and undoubtedly to assess my skills and experience as well). He appeared committed to devoting whatever time was needed. The meeting had no official ending time. He was not preoccupied and gave me his full attention. He spoke directly, honestly, and without pretense. There was a bit of an aw-shucks air about him that came across through his common way of speaking and his laid-back body language. He was a Texas native and it showed. Through these simple behaviors, he demonstrated an authenticity that put me at ease and a sense that he understood my feelings.

He shared more about who he was than I expected and disclosed his feelings about the acquisition — and how it affected people. He also shared his dreams for what the new organization could become as we merged the two businesses. On a personal level, he talked a bit about his own family and personal life — and how they would be affected. He shared just enough to let me know he trusted me and wanted my trust in return. He was willing to let his guard down somewhat and be vulnerable. It was clear that personal relationships and family were important to him as he went about his business roles.

Clearly, a high level of intelligence was present beneath his casual style — he knew how to run companies and merge them very well. I respected his knowledge and experience, and trusted his competence. I believed he was well intentioned and would follow through in finding the right spot for me.

In direct terms, he let me know that I would be a valued part of the new company. In his mind, the team and the organization came first and foremost. If he got the right people in place, with the appropriate strategy, the business results would follow (and they did). He made me feel that I was a respected colleague on equal footing with him, even though he would be my boss, and that whether I was male or female (in a male-oriented business environment) made no difference at all. I felt connected emotionally to him, to the new company, and the emerging opportunity. I was committed to helping the business succeed and helping him navigate the challenging path ahead (personal communication, 2017).

THE POWER OF EMOTION

This story, relayed during our interviews, is about a woman at a career crossroads. It exemplifies the importance of immediate impressions and the ability to connect on both an emotional plane and intellectual plane. If you don't connect on an affective level, especially when the other person is anxious, upset, or emotional in another way, he or she may miss the main points you wish to communicate. In the story, the CEO was delivering favorable news, making a motivating conversation easier. When the situation is unfavorable, emotions such as anger and distrust often interfere with understanding and processing of the intended message, and ultimately job performance (Pervez, 2010). Such negative emotions have a spillover effect on decision-making, teamwork, interpersonal relations, creativity, and leadership (Pervez, 2010). Emotions have a profound influence on behavior. For catalysts to be effective, they must be able to connect when things are going well and when they are not.

Empathy is about finding echoes of another person in yourself.
— Mohsin Hamid (The New Yorker, 2012)

When the team is on a roll and members are high-fiving, it's relatively easy for catalysts to connect emotionally with others and spur them on. Psychiatrist and bestselling author, Edward Hallowell, shows why positive, energizing emotions are critical to inspiring people's best performance and how engagement is essential to spurring their best work (Hallowell 2015).

It's more challenging to connect emotionally when others are upset or the team is experiencing setbacks. It's in these situations where the skills that underlie the ability to connect emotionally are exceptionally valuable. The objective is to transform negative emotions into positive energy. This requires an understanding of three types of empathy; each begins with a solid understanding of self. Jean Decety, at the University of Chicago, describes them:

- *Cognitive empathy* allows you to sense how someone else thinks about the world. This helps your messages to be heard.

- *Emotional empathy* demonstrates your ability to accurately read the emotions of your peers or your staff and will enable you to relate with their personal experiences.

- *Empathic concern* is the ability to sense or anticipate what someone else needs and express that you care about those needs. Reaching out to them will build stronger relationships (Decety, 2010).

Think about a time when you were in high spirits. How would you want others to connect with you? Conversely, think about a time when you were feeling low. How would you have liked others to relate to you? How can you use those insights to connect emotionally with others on your team?

The field of emotional intelligence as researched by Daniel Goleman (1995) focuses first and foremost upon an active understanding of self. His research demonstrates the importance of understanding your own emotions in order to effectively relate to others. He describes a nuanced and continuous process. His book has become a primer for leaders who wish to connect effectively with others to achieve results. Goleman begins this process by showing you how to understand yourself through self-awareness and self-regulation. He suggests that only after mastering the self can you more accurately interpret the emotions of others.

Underlying your emotional credibility with others may be an enhanced willingness to share your emotions more readily, often to the point of some vulnerability. The connection comes from your understanding of them and whether things are going well or if the individual is under stress. The balance of this chapter encourages you to explore paths to empathetic behavior and offers guidance.

THREE PERFORMANCE CHALLENGES

The following are the primary challenges that confront catalysts:

1. How to prevent or alleviate performance-suppressing emotions.

2. How to turn around performance-suppressing emotions.

3. How to activate and perpetuate performance-elevating emotions.

Each of these is accomplished by connecting emotionally in different ways as discussed in the following sections.

Preventing or Mitigating Performance-Suppressing Emotions

On teams and in organizations of all shapes and sizes, people sometimes react to circumstances in negative ways, often because it affects them personally, because they believe decisions are ill-advised, because they are concerned about how others will be impacted, or for any number of other reasons. Whatever the reason, negative emotions such as anger, hostility, exasperation, fear, anxiety, isolation, humiliation, and others are dispiriting. To avert or lessen these reactions, and their possible negative impact on performance, catalysts often:

Get out in front of them. In anticipation of how someone may react, meet with them to discuss what is about to happen and seek their thoughts and suggestions. If appropriate, involve the person in addressing challenges, anticipating and managing implications, and problem-solving.

Preserve the person's self-esteem or feelings of self-worth. Explain you are discussing the matter with them ahead of time, in confidence, because you value who they are and what they do for the organization.

Demonstrate empathy. Empathy entails showing that one understands or can feel what others are experiencing from their perspective. Depending on the severity of the emotions, this may be the first step you take with the person. The easiest and most direct way to show empathy is to simply acknowledge what you believe the other person is feeling. Examples:

> *"You seem very frustrated by this situation."*
>
> *"I see that you are upset by what happened."*
>
> *"I can understand why you're angry."*
>
> *"I realize this is a let down for you."*

Statements such as these tend to defuse emotions and often have a calming effect. Even if, from the other person's perspective, you have misidentified the emotion and they correct you, perhaps by saying, "I'm not upset, I'm just very disappointed," your empathetic response still conveys an emotional connection. You can simply reply by saying something like, "I can understand why and I would be as well. Is there anything I can do to help?"

Turning Around Performance-Suppressing Emotions

The first step in turning negative emotions into positive ones is to mitigate them when they occur, especially through expressing empathy, preserving self-esteem, and offering genuine support. To transform feelings and restore or enhance performance levels:

- Intercede early to address negative emotions before they fester, grow, and infect others.

- Build on the positives. Identify and discuss silver linings to build a positive outlook, put issues into perspective, and ascertain possibilities.

- Provide a ladder out of the trap:
  - Suggest training and other developmental opportunities.

  - Identify positive role models.

  - Discuss the person's job fit and whether they would be better in a different role.

  - Follow up and reinforce positive change or progress.

  - Propose standards for future performance.

One-to-One Discussion Tactics

- Describe in a neutral way the concern about the negative emotions. Be prepared to discuss specific behavioral examples of the person's display of performance-suppressing emotions. When you do, identify the circumstances in which it occurred, what he or she did or said, and the impact on others and the team — which may include morale, interpersonal conflict, and team processes and results.

- Listen to the person's explanation and point of view without interrupting. Acknowledge appropriate points. Don't dispute what is said and don't let organizational or other people's issues excuse his or her negative emotions.

- Recognize and reinforce what the person does well.

- Ask what he or she sees as solutions or ways of putting it behind them. Ask how they might express themselves or act differently.

- Coach as needed.

- Remain positive and constructive yourself. Your objective should be to develop solutions with the person and help him or her climb out of emotional negativity.

Activating and Perpetuating Performance-Elevating Emotions

Sustained catalytic performance entails getting beyond performance-suppressing emotions and sparking and sustaining performance-elevating emotions. "Rah rah" enthusiasm may be fine on occasion, especially to pump up sports teams before a big game, but it's momentary. It's not the kind of positive, ongoing connection that generates sustained performance-elevating emotions. These are developed in more subtle ways, ways that instill deeper and more meaningful psychological connections.

Catalytic leaders and team members inspire and engage in ways that draw out internal motivations. These emotional connections are created in many different manners. They tap into the well of needs each of us has — needs for purpose, fulfillment, involvement, achievement, influence, belief, and affiliation, as well as needs to feel valued, appreciated, recognized, worthy, and to be part of something greater than ourselves.

To inspire performance-elevating emotions — in essence, sustained catalytic passion:

Involve team members so they feel invested in the journey. Engage the others in establishing an aspirational vision and path forward. Get everyone's fingerprints on the plan. Remind team members frequently about the team's overall purpose and the reason why it's important.

Emphasize the need to serve customers well and that the team's success is linked to customer success. Share stories about the difference the team has made in the lives of others. Strike emotional chords.

Demonstrate your own passion for the team's objectives. Talk it up. Spread it — promote its contagion.

Include team members in setting high expectations for what the team can achieve and what it stands for. Engage them in setting stretch goals — goals that are achievable but require extra effort and commitment to accomplish.

Seek team members' help in solving problems and addressing team challenges. Set expectations in the form of hard work, time, and overall dedication.

Publicly recognize and express appreciation for the efforts and accomplishments of others in conversations, meetings, presentations, e-mails, and other written communications. Tell stories that spotlight the contribution and impact of other team members.

Show humility. When recognized yourself, illustrate how your contributions and impact are part of the overall team effort. Magnanimously spread the credit to others.

Talk about the meaning and personal benefits of success — of achieving the goals the team set out to achieve and how reaching them will reflect positively on each team member.

Use measured progress as a way to sustain drive and keep others emotionally engaged. Use milestones to motivate and instill a belief in what can and will be achieved.

Aspirational Practices

- Inspire with a can-do attitude, a "we are all in this together" spirit.

- Relax and laugh together. The strongest emotional connections may occur when taking breathers, letting your hair down as a group, and getting to know each other on a personal level.

- Dream with your team and each team member about future possibilities. Paint compelling pictures of what is possible.

- Encourage a spirit of cooperation. Avoid talking about who is better than whom.

- Celebrate both team and individual successes. Recognize accomplishments.

These practices develop emotional ties to both the initiator — the catalyst — and the endeavor. They channel intrinsic motivations, build commitment and ownership, and boost efforts to excel. Connecting emotionally helps messages get through and prevents them from being rejected before they are really heard.

Connecting emotionally is crucial in the case of both employees and customers. The company strives to make emotional connections with the customer and their products; the team leader strives to make emotional connections with their employees. Many of the practices we've listed above serve to accomplish this. This in turn activates positive emotion-driven performance.

A vivid example of this can be found in the marketing techniques Steve Jobs used to promote Apple products. Jobs excited prospective customers about the idea of what Apple products could do, whether it was transforming their computer experience or how they listened to music. With the iPod, he didn't simply sell you a device that could play music — he provided a means for changing your relationship with music. With the Mac, he didn't simply sell you a product to replace your personal computer. You may remember the 1984, George Orwell-themed television commercial Apple produced. That advertisement was devoid of content you might think a rational computer buyer might want to know. It did not mention price, size, features, or processing speed — and only used the word computer once.

What it did contain was *emotion*. The messaging tapped into the prevailing emotions of consumers and was designed to elicit personal reactions and evoke an emotional connection at the product-customer level.

Catalytic leaders, in a parallel way, create emotional connections with their employees. They build a strong internal brand identity with their associates. In the eyes of their employees, the top three most-beloved companies are Salesforce.com, Southwest Airlines, and Anadarko Petroleum Corporation (Strauss, 2016). These companies enjoy extremely high employee loyalty and dedication to achieving results.

A recent example can be found at the Community Healthcare System in Indiana. The organization combined three distinct areas — Patient Experience, Employee Experience (including Human Resources), and Marketing/Communications — into one department in recognition of the importance of providing a positive experience for both patients and employees. The driving philosophy behind this was to create emotional connections that emanated from the organization to staff, which in turn strengthened their relationships with patients. The intention was to improve overall brand loyalty.

CONCLUSION

We began this chapter with an interviewee who was at a crossroads in her career and who benefitted from the immediate emotional connection that her new boss made with her. Perhaps her boss was naturally predisposed to being a thoughtful communicator and emotional connector — understanding her worries and concerns. But you don't need to have this intrinsic capability. Making emotional connections can be learned, fostered, and improved so that you can both alleviate performance-suppressing emotions and strengthen performance-elevating drivers.

Take a moment to reflect on your own behavior, do you:

- Acknowledge your own emotions in interactions with other team members and understand how they influence your responses?

- Understand how positive expectations for yourself and others can help build strong connections?

- Share your feelings appropriately?

- Acknowledge the emotions of others?

- Refer to the inventory of techniques in this chapter for handling performance-suppressing emotions?

- Engage in behaviors that elevate performance-enhancing emotions?

5

DEVELOPS CAMARADERIE

Definition: Establishes a positive rapport and fosters constructive interactions.

Counter Behaviors: Adversarial, creates conflict, divisive, discredits others, cliquish. Sees others as rivals rather than partners.

CAMARADERIE AT McDONALD'S

We introduced you to the special nature of the Indianapolis area McDonald's crew in Chapter 3, "Invigorates with Optimism." Team camaraderie also propelled its stellar performance. We discovered through our interviews and on-site observations that crew members were dedicated to serving customers, ensuring satisfaction, and making the store as successful as possible through their combined efforts. We saw how they helped each other in friendly and constructive ways — and most seemed to genuinely like each other. They fit into the store's culture and actively promoted it. They supported each other through positive and constructive interactions, demonstrating mutual respect — even when correcting errors in the heat of the lunch crush and coaching on how to increase work speed and effectiveness. Additionally, friendships were forged that contributed to an esprit de corps. Cohesive fellowship helped drive the crew's high performance.

Camaraderie is the glue at the center of teamwork.

Andrew Carnegie has been widely quoted as saying, "Teamwork is the ability to work together toward a common vision," and is the "ability to

direct individual accomplishments toward organizational objectives. It is the
fuel that allows common people to attain uncommon results."

WHAT CREATES CAMARADERIE?

Camaraderie is the glue at the center of teamwork. It contributes to catalytic
performance when it encompasses four key elements (Feehi, Boateng, &
Mensah, 2016):

- Common commitment to a purpose.

- Promotion of a healthy team culture.

- Mutual respect among team members.

- Workplace friendship.

Each of these plays a crucial part in developing camaraderie and creating
and sustaining a catalytic dynamic.

Common Commitment to a Purpose

The mission of every team is to work together to achieve common
objectives — whether it's a sports team, business team, music ensemble,
community service group, organizational committee, project team, or some
other collective with a purpose.

> An organization or team's real culture — its "values, attitudes, and
> beliefs" — is demonstrated through its actual collective behavior
> patterns.
>
> — Taylor, 2013

A pivotal factor in a team's success is the dedication of its members to
pull together, as a cohesive unit, to achieve shared goals. That commitment
binds the team members together in a common cause and fuels camaraderie —
especially when each person views his or her role as a significant element in
the team's success. Human catalysts strive to create this dynamic, in large
part by prioritizing team goals over personal objectives and encouraging
other members to do the same.

Healthy Culture

An organization or team's real culture — its "values, attitudes, and beliefs" — is demonstrated through its actual collective behavior patterns (Taylor, 2013). It's not what may be written on a poster or advocated in a speech. Those are statements of the desired culture — what the organization or team might be striving to become, not the reality.

A stark example of how the reality may be very different from the statements can be found in the infamous example of Enron Corporation. Enron (as cited in Sacramento State, n.d.) listed its values as follows:

Respect: We treat others as we would like to be treated ourselves. We do not tolerate abusive or disrespectful treatment. Ruthlessness, callousness, and arrogance don't belong here.

Integrity: We work with customers and prospects openly, honestly, and sincerely. When we say we will do something, we will do it; when we say we cannot or will not do something, then we won't do it.

Communication: We have an obligation to communicate. Here, we take the time to talk with one another ... and to listen. We believe that information is meant to move and that information moves people.

Excellence: We are satisfied with nothing less than the very best in everything we do. We will continue to raise the bar for everyone. The great fun here will be for all of us to discover just how good we can really be.

The reality was extremely different. The company's notorious unethical practices and misrepresentations created an artificial energy crisis in California. Enron defrauded their customers and investors. They lied about the company's financial health. They kept regulators in the dark. Ultimately, the company collapsed. Thousands of lives and careers were torpedoed in the process.

Whether leaders or team members, catalysts actively embody and promote positive values, attitudes, and beliefs — and strive to get others on board as well. The cultural dynamics (the practices and processes for how the mission is undertaken) that flow from such efforts contribute to team cohesion. They serve as a unifying force and help forge the unit's identity — important elements necessary for the creation of team camaraderie. A human catalyst acts not only to develop camaraderie with one or two others but to also accelerate its creation within the entire team — so it becomes an underlying and sustaining part of the culture.

When the horserace for key roles in an organization becomes intense, camaraderie may suffer. The dynamics of the team, the relationships among key players, can become much more difficult. But the competitive drive needn't lead to dysfunction. During our interview with the CEO of an industrial corporation, he commented, "Paul and Ricardo both now know they won't make it onto our senior management team, but they play very important roles and they know it. We explained that they wouldn't be managing people and they accepted that. People management was not among their strengths. When they were freed from that pressure, they gained greater respect from others for their expertise, knowledge, and experience. They let go of their need to be stars with titles and authority. They became cohesive influences in the organization. Their expertise as project leaders, mentors, and go-to professionals cultivated relationships that made each of their teams more effective." (personal communication, 2016)

Michael Mankins writes in the *Harvard Business Review* (*HBR*) that "winning cultures aren't just about affiliation; they are also unashamedly about results." (Mankins, 2013) Mankins discusses several corporate examples, including how Ford Motor Company turned around a "decades-long slide" by creating a "working together" culture that "refocused and reenergized the company, and how Herb Kelleher's leadership at Southwest Airlines developed a 'culture of employee empowerment and cost containment' instrumental in transforming it from a small regional carrier to one of most respected and profitable."

Mankins explains, "Culture doesn't always produce great results." The reason is because many companies view culture as simply "a way to make people feel good about where they work and not as a way to help employees — hence the organization — perform better." (Mankins, 2013) The two must work hand in hand.

> *Human catalysts help create and enhance a winning culture, and in doing so, build and strengthen camaraderie.*

Distilled from the research that Mankins and Bain & Company conducted with over 400 senior executives are seven cultural performance attributes, as described in the *HBR* article:

1. **Honesty and integrity** in all interactions with employees, customers, suppliers, and other stakeholders.

2. **Performance-focused** rewards, development, and other talent-management practices.

3. **Accountable and owner-like:** Roles, responsibilities, and authority should reinforce ownership over work and results.

4. **Collaboration:** Recognition that the best ideas come from the exchange and sharing of ideas between individuals and teams.

5. **Agile and adaptive:** The organization is able to turn on a dime when necessary and adapt to changes in the external environment.

6. **Innovative:** Employees push the envelope in terms of new ways of thinking.

7. **Oriented toward winning:** There is strong ambition focused on objective measures of success, either versus the competition or against some absolute standard of excellence.

Mankins (2013) notes that few high-performing organizations display all of these attributes, but most are strong in at least three or four, especially those that are most relevant for their business. Also essential is that the attributes reinforce behaviors that propel performance and that they align with the organization's overarching strategy.

Human catalysts help create and enhance a winning culture, and in doing so, build and strengthen camaraderie. They model the behaviors, they encourage others to as well, and they weave them into what they do and say. A healthy culture is key to forging a compelling organizational identity that develops pride, affiliation, and passion, and in so doing creates a peformance-focused purpose. It's also an amazing way to attract top talent.

Mutual Respect among Team Members

According to Dr. Richard Clark, professor of Educational Psychology and Technology at the University of Southern California, "... confidence in each other's expertise is the only factor that accounts for their success in high pressure situations." (Clark, 2005) Whether it's the only factor or a highly critical one, confidence or mutual respect among team members is essential to success. Albert Bandura's extensive assessment of sports team research concludes, "... in pressure-packed, over-time matches where contestants are evenly matched and a mistake brings a sudden-death defeat ... perceived (group) efficacy emerges as the sole determinant of overtime performance." (cited in Clark, 2005) Bandura "goes on to suggest that the same is true for all teams that are in competitive situations." (cited in Clark, 2005)

How do catalysts promote mutual respect? Beyond encouraging it in daily interactions, Clark identifies four other practices:

- Helping weaker team members believe that their effort is vital to team success.

- Supporting a shared belief in the cooperative capabilities of the team.

- Holding individual team members accountable for their contributions to the team effort.

- Directing the team's competitive spirit outside the team and the organization.

Mutual respect is an essential ingredient in both strengthening cohesiveness and camaraderie and is especially critical when teams must produce under pressure.

A marketing professional at a major art museum described the camaraderie that occurs among her team members, especially when they are up against tight deadlines or in the midst of a crisis. During the interview in 2015 she explained, "It is a three musketeer attitude; it is one for all and all for one! Everyone on the team brings this feeling of companionship to work each and every day. No one needs to stand out. Everyone rallies around whoever the project driver is at a given point in time — the person best able to lead us through our critical path. If needed, they come in early; they stay late for the good of the team and their teammates. No one needs to be in the spotlight." (personal communication, 2015)

Workplace Friendships

Workplace friendships often entail having one or more coworkers with whom one can trust and confide, share stories, discuss work-related issues, ask for unofficial help or coaching, meet for lunch, or socialize after work.

Beyond the personal benefits, workplace friendships have a positive impact on individual and organizational performance.

In Gallup's Q12 Employee Engagement Survey, workplace friendship was found to be one of twelve core elements that "best predict employee and workplace performance" (Gallup.com, n.d.). Seventy-five percent of those with a good workplace friend intended to remain with the company for at least another year (Lee & Ok, 2011). By comparison, only 51% of respondents who reported not having one claimed they would stay.

These and other studies have consistently reported that workplace friendships improve employee work-related attitudes and behaviors that, in turn, enhance organizational outcomes. Earlier research points to greater organizational performance when workplace friends help each other with tasks and build each other's morale. They have fewer communication issues, which translate into greater effort and higher productivity (Bandura, 1982).

We have all seen bursts of camaraderie and celebration when sports teams win championships. It may be an emotional release after a long pressure-filled journey together to achieve a shared dream. Yet the true test of effective camaraderie is how group members behave when the team is struggling, when it's in a slump, or nothing seems to be going well. It's during these times that conflict among team members is more likely to arise and to be more intense and become dysfunctional. Enmity can shatter cohesion. On the other hand, constructive conflict can have the opposite effect. It can bring unstated issues to light, heighten awareness about the impact of problems or deficiencies in performance, and spark discussions about how the team can resolve problems and improve. It may also stimulate the team to identify and explore fresh perspectives and develop innovative solutions. It all depends on the nature of the conflict and how people respond to it. When conflict becomes personal and highly charged emotionally, camaraderie and unity suffer. When the conflict is centered squarely and neutrally on how to address a problem, fix a process, or achieve an objective, the probability of enhancing team companionship and cohesion is improved.

Camaraderie for the sake of camaraderie bears little fruit.

Catalytic performance depends on camaraderie in combination with other catalytic competencies. To contribute to organizational success, companionship must be goal-oriented. Camaraderie for the sake of camaraderie bears little fruit. As J. Ross (2005) reports in a study of 20 corporate executive teams, team camaraderie is healthy, helpful, and productive until relationships are prioritized over organizational goals — and it's frequently the goals that are sacrificed. People avoid difficult conversations, strong opinions are not aired, and performance that falls short is pardoned for the sake of fellowship.

For mission-focused camaraderie to become catalytic, infuse it with the four attributes listed at the beginning of this chapter: fostering a common commitment to a purpose, promoting a healthy team culture, facilitating mutual respect among team members, and developing performance-oriented workplace friendships.

CONCLUSION

Catalytic team members strengthen the bonds of camaraderie. Many of us spend far more time with people at work than we do socializing with our families. As such, developing companionship with your colleagues and contributing to their success adds to their job enjoyment and fulfillment, as well as your own.

Formichelli (2016) describes how this takes place among the restaurants operated by an Applebee's franchisee. The franchisee hosts what he calls The Top Apple Chef Competition. Employees prepare new dishes. Each dish is judged and winners receive awards and prizes. While this activity focuses on individuals, entire stores get involved. Employees who submit dishes have conversations and swap ideas with nonparticipants for weeks prior to the event. Winners move on to represent their store in an advanced round. They do so with a sense of pride and camaraderie with other restaurant employees who were engaged in the process — such as teams of tasters and those who may have shared favorite family recipes.

As an engaging CEO mentioned to us: "I put a lot of value in having people in our organization who are fun to be around, who have a good sense of humor, who can connect on a personal level with others, and who can spark the team with high energy!" (personal communication).

Take a moment to reflect on your own behavior, do you:

- Focus on the relationships of all the team members, not just yours?

- Look to understand people as they are — develop and show empathy?

- Help the team identify a shared sense of purpose?

- Balance team relationships with a drive toward team results?

- Refocus conflicts on constructive action? Use them as vehicles to solve problems and breed innovation?

6

PUTS THE TEAM'S GOALS AND THE ORGANIZATION'S MISSION BEFORE PERSONAL INTERESTS

Definition: Prioritizes team success and process over personal goals. Selfless; does what it takes to achieve results by focusing on overarching organizational goals.

Counter Behavior: Promotes self; puts own interests and performance ahead of the team's mission. Focuses on self to the exclusion of others and the team.

IGNITING A MOVEMENT

During a long nighttime stakeout ... in the spring of 1980, U.S. Customs Agent Tommy Austin tells Arizona Department of Public Safety [DPS] Officer Ron Cox his problem.

His wife's friend has a small son named Chris who is probably going to die of leukemia. The seven-year-old boy yearns to be a police officer ... Austin asks Cox if maybe DPS can do something.

Cox takes the request to DPS spokesman Allan Schmidt, who asks DPS Director Ralph Milstead. He gives Schmidt carte blanche to grant Chris' wish.

"None of us had any idea what we were getting into at the time," Schmidt will recall 30 years later. He draws other people in: Officer Jim Eaves will bring his patrol car, and Officer Frank Shankwitz his motorcycle, to meet the DPS helicopter flying Chris to headquarters. On April 29, Chris

comes from Scottsdale Memorial Hospital ... That's when Lt. Col. Dick Schaefer gives the boy a "Smokey Bear" hat and one of his own old badges ... Chris becomes Arizona's first and only honorary DPS officer.

Everyone who meets the beaming boy chewing bubble gum wants to help. ...

Cox and Eaves go to John's Uniforms ... and order one [in] Chris' size ... Shankwitz sets up cones for Chris to steer his battery-powered motorcycle through to qualify for a motorcycle officer's wings ...

When they return the next day to present the wings to Chris, he's gone back into the hospital. With his DPS gifts all around him ... Chris gives a last smile for the men who have done so much for him in such a short time.

"He was only seven years, 269 days old when he died. But he taught me about being a man. Even though he was only a boy."... [said] Tommy Austin, Make-A-Wish® cofounder and retired U.S. Customs agent. (Make-A-Wish®, http://wish.org/about-us/our-story/, 2017)

Not all of us have quite as dramatic a story as Tommy Austin, who after his time with Chris, cofounded the Make-A-Wish® Foundation. But this story brings to life the idea of putting self-interest aside to fully focus on achieving a mission — in this case, the wish of a young boy.

Tommy Austin displayed behaviors that capture the essence of putting team before self.

He saw a specific need and passionately committed his own resources to meeting it; he rallied other generous hearts on the team to join the cause; he understood what success would look like for this young man and charted a clear path to achieve it; when faced with a potentially derailing obstacle, he pulled the team together to adjust their course and meet the needs of a very special boy.

Make-A-Wish® did not exist when Tommy Austin was moved to making Chris' dreams come true. But his passion served as the spark that inspired many others to establish the team, the organization that thrives today.

After the wish, those involved were inspired and eager to bring that same hope, strength, and joy to more children. Their simple idea led to the establishment of the world's largest wish-granting organization, now operating in nearly 50 countries and granting a wish every 34 minutes.

Make-A-Wish® has extended its mission by leveraging strategic partnerships with other organizations. The magical relationship Make-A-Wish® has formed with Disney® on a global scale began with Frank "Bopsy"

Salazar, the first official Disney Make-A-Wish® child. Like Chris, he was a seven-year-old boy in the United States, diagnosed with leukemia, who revered people in uniform. His dream of being a firefighter was granted, and he became the first of a long line of Wish children to visit a Disney Theme Park.

There's no denying that catalysts put team and mission first.

THE IMPORTANCE OF PUTTING TEAM BEFORE SELF

Can you think of an occasion when you were motivated to help someone? And to extend that idea, can you think of an occasion when you were motivated to help someone, but in the process, you lost out on something you sought personally? Perhaps it was a missed bonus, a lost opportunity to perform a solo, or failing to get the full credit you deserved on an important project. The willingness to put team above self is a critical behavior that drives collaboration and establishes you as a catalytic leader.

In a symphony orchestra, the conductor has a choice as to how to work with world-class musicians to encourage them to play seamlessly together as one unit, one sound. The mission of a team of 75-plus musicians is to achieve a precise balance of sound and tempo in their interpretation of the musical score — to the delight of the audience. In this situation, the trombone section was not well balanced with the other musicians on stage; they were too loud and were overpowering the strings. Jack, an experienced conductor who is well known nationally, had two choices as to how to gain the cooperation of the trombone section to focus on the team's mission. Option one: "Trombones, hey folks, tone it down a bit; it's not all about you in this portion of the score. I need you to back off a bit." Option two: "Trombone friends, I'm always struck by how 'live' this symphony hall is, how well the sound travels. I need your help in balancing the sound so that we achieve the balance we need in this portion of the piece. Could you play with the same feeling and intensity, but with just a bit less volume? I know it's going to create a terrific overall effect for this piece."

An experienced conductor, Jack chose the latter — more emotionally intelligent — approach that made the trombone section more likely to put the group's needs before their own. The result was that Jack achieved, as he nearly always does, a wonderful, full-orchestra sound consistent with the mission and the effect on the audience that the composer had in mind.

He skillfully invited his colleagues to join him on a noble mission in service of beautiful music, and they were eager to oblige.

Before going further in this discussion, let's consider a selfless act that you have completed. Can you articulate why you might have done something to help another that cost you something? It may be something deeply personal that reveals how you think of yourself, relative to the team and others. Your sacrifice may not take the dramatic form of starting a non-profit organization the size and scope of Make-A-Wish®, but the drive to contribute to others and the team is a very powerful force indeed.

> One thing I believe to the fullest is that if you think and achieve as a team, the individual accolades will take care of themselves. Talent wins games, but teamwork and intelligence win championships.
> — Michael Jordan (cited in Favale, 2013)

SELF VERSUS OTHER OR SELF AND OTHER

As individuals, we are naturally highly motivated by our own desires and wants, that is, our self-interest. As an indication of how powerful the concept of self-interest is, consider that it is a bedrock principle in Adam Smith's popular economic theories as described in *Wealth of Nations* (1776). This message is stated plainly by Smith, who contends that markets operate best when two conditions are met: that competition exists and *that we individually pursue rational self-interest.* Stated another way, pursuing what is best for ourselves is not only normal, but it is also desirable — when rational.

In the context of evidence by Smith and other writers and researchers who followed him, there is support that humans are deeply self-interested. How do catalytic leaders overcome this tendency? Let's examine that in the next section.

LEADERSHIP, SACRIFICE, AND THE GREATER GOOD

While it may sound counterintuitive, leadership requires sacrificing degrees of autonomy. Leaders are responsible not just for themselves but also for their team. They have greater accountability for producing results. They must manage issues and team dynamics. Their success depends on the team achieving or exceeding expectations. Therefore, they must put the team and its mission above personal interests. They have less freedom, not more.

Catalytic team members strive to see things from their leader's perspective, and to make that person's accountabilities their own — going beyond the boundaries of their specific responsibilities — to help the team succeed in however they can. They make sacrifices and put their own needs secondary to the team's needs.

Perhaps no other set of institutions is as well known for its emphasis on putting team and mission above self than the branches of the U.S. military. In the U.S. Army's Creed, soldiers are instilled with the ethic of always placing the mission first and never leaving a fallen comrade (Army Values, n.d.). These are challenging values to uphold, especially when one is in harm's way or one's own life is in peril. Knowing fellow soldiers have embraced the same principles and will act accordingly is a powerful cohesive force.

Chief Master Sergeant Jacob P.E. Dunbar of the U.S. Air Force Special Operations Command describes some of the personal sacrifices team members should make for the good of the team and its mission. He offers advice for subduing "pride to ensure the overall advancement of the team or institution." (Dunbar, 2015)

Dunbar's Rules

- Do what needs to be done even if you don't like it or feel it's degrading. This takes a lot of heart. Although your inclination is telling you "don't," you have to find all the reasons to "do."

- Focus on the team's goals and purpose, even when working for someone who gets on your nerves or you think is incompetent. Though you can't help but notice the individual's flaws, keep your eyes on bigger things.

- Remain professional when someone is disrespectful. The first thought could be to retaliate, which harms cohesiveness and the mission and often makes the situation worse. Keep advancing, because every time you get sidetracked by petty matters, you lose focus and stop momentum. Be a role model for demonstrating the right priorities.

- Compromise personal ideas for the good of the team. Most of us have deep-rooted views of how work should be done and how people should act in various situations. How you see things through your lenses can be drastically different from others, but that does not mean any of the ideas are bad. It is more about what is best for the team. Even though you think your thoughts are more profound and beneficial than others, it does not matter once a decision has been made by the team. Be humble and loyal enough to put the institution first rather than your feelings.

- Humble leadership requires considerable self-discipline. It requires you at times to subordinate your pride, desires, and views. Each individual has the choice to check out or stay in the game. Remaining says a lot about a person. It does not make you weak. It takes more strength to keep leading than to quit. As Dunbar explains, "[H]umble leadership is ... about advancing the team even if you have to make some concessions."

- Do not let personality issues, petty irritants, and ego distract from achieving important objectives. In essence, he is saying, rise above them.

WHAT IS SELFLESSNESS?

Let's look at selfless behavior and its motivation. The best examples usually involve a situation where it is necessary that you give up something of your own to provide for someone else. Also known as *altruism*, some critics contend that you can never *really* do something altruistically; there is always some aspect of self-interest in every act. Some may debate that premise, but for our purposes, simply imagine parents that go hungry so that their child can eat. The needs or even the survival of another requires personal sacrifice. It requires altruistic behavior. The notion is that "the world is bigger than you." This is something Brad Stevens believes is the life lesson that sports teaches children (PCA Development Zone®, Resource Center, n.d.).

Selfless behavior is considered by some researchers to be embedded in our human nature. Lieberman (1994) describes the three capabilities that make humans unique:

- The capacity for cognition.
- The capacity of language.
- The capacity to engage in selfless behavior.

The last capacity is a hallmark of catalytic behavior.

Drivers of Selflessness

In studies of evolutionary biology, selfless behavior or altruism is noted as being entirely consistent with Darwinian theories of natural selection (Okasha, 2013). For some, this may be counterintuitive because the act of reducing your own calories isn't likely to improve your chances of survival. Yet it is precisely a fact that means sacrificial behavior will help those around you to survive. Passing DNA that values sacrificial behavior will help those around you to survive over generations.

Consider the experiments that included chimps. Two were housed next to each other with a screen through which they could see each other. One chimpanzee had to choose between two differently colored tokens from a bin — one of which represented a pro-social option, the other a selfish option. The pro-social option would cause both chimpanzees to receive a piece of banana wrapped in paper. The selfish option only rewarded the ape that made the choice. In this study that included seven adult female chimps placed into various pairs, the scientists found all the apes showed a definite preference for the pro-social option. "For me, the most important finding is that like us, chimpanzees take into account the needs and wishes of others," researcher Victoria Horner, a comparative psychologist at Emory University, told LiveScience (Choi, 2011).

An additional powerful motivator of team or mission-oriented behavior is the feeling of belonging to the tribe or the group. Whether a sports team, a musical ensemble, a political party, or church congregation, our identities can be closely wrapped up in the team. Your identity may be deeply connected to others, and through those connections, we find personal meaning. This personal identification with a particular group of others can be a powerful driver of selfless behavior. For example, Netflix has an organizational culture and values that are the mantra for all employees. This culture focuses on selflessness and incorporates aspects of it into each employee's behavior, who is challenged to:

- Seek what is best for Netflix, rather than best for yourself or your group.

- Be ego-less when searching for the best ideas.

- Make time to help colleagues.

- Share information openly and proactively.

The factors of innate altruism, social identity, and the norms of a group can drive selfless behavior. Netflix has been referred to as the company that reinvented human resources (McCord, 2014).

Selflessness Aimed at the New Teammate

Another reason the Butler men's basketball team was so successful in 2010 and 2011 involves the relationship between Gordon Hayward, currently a highly successful NBA player, and Willie Veasley. When Gordon Hayward joined the Butler University men's basketball team in 2008, he was noticed by a junior guard/small forward named Willie Veasley. Veasley was a hard-nosed player who seemed to be in the right place at the right time. He was looking to gain significant playing time and an opportunity to score points in ways that he hadn't as a freshman and sophomore. However, Willie epitomized selflessness in putting the team's success ahead of his own personal performance and stats, doing everything he could to help Hayward develop rapidly as a key element of the Bulldogs' team.

Sports writer, Graham Couch explored this phenomenon in more depth, relaying that Veasely's statistics were as modest and unassuming as the small Northwest Illinois town that raised him at ten points and four rebounds per game. Gordon Hayward commented about Veasely, "He's just kind of the glue that holds us all together. ... He does so many things that don't get noticed that help you win as a team. If you were a coach, you'd recognize it more. Coach has showed me clips on it, just little things — he'll set a screen to get me open when he could have just rolled and popped open himself or he'll make the extra pass." (cited in Couch, 2010)

Veasley's impact on the Butler's men's basketball team was best told by those who were eager to state his worth — and by one number — 117 (Couch, 2010). This is his number of career victories. Along with his teammate Nick Rogers, that was the most in the history of Butler basketball. "Most people don't recognize him and don't see him, and he doesn't get enough credit for what he does for our team," echoed junior Matt Howard (cited in Couch, 2010), adding, "He's been incredible defensively all year. And he adds versatility to our team both defensively and offensively. And at 6'3" — which you wouldn't expect out of somebody that size to be able to guard and play so many different positions." (cited in Couch, 2010)

But he can and he has. As a true freshman, playing with a broken hand, Veasley found himself matched up against 6'10" Indiana forward D.J. White, and tipped in the go-ahead bucket in one of the first of his many wins. Since, he's guarded point guards and centers and everything in between while playing in four NCAA tournaments, two Sweet 16s, and helping Butler to its first Final Four.

In this article, Butler coach Brad Stevens said, "Going out as the winningness player in Butler history is fitting for Willie, because Willie will do anything you ask him to do to help your team win. I call him our Shane Battier." (cited in Couch, 2010)

CONCLUSION

Veasley sparked collaboration and team success based on his ability to selflessly put his teammates before his own need for notoriety and points. In our research, we find that this is typical of the most influential catalysts on teams across all three sectors: sports, business, and the arts. Individual commitment to overarching goals, and putting them ahead of personal interests, takes many forms.

Take a moment to reflect on your own behavior, do you:

- See the big picture clearly; embrace it with passion?

- Understand what accomplishment of the team's mission will look like if you are wildly successful?

- Identify new members of the team that can become spark plugs for highly successful team performance?

- Identify selfless people around you and model their behavior, and reciprocate selfless acts done on your behalf?

- Maintain a clear line-of-sight between your job and its responsibilities and the team's objectives and the organization's mission?

- Ensure each activity is linked to the mission? When it's unclear if one is, whether your own or another members, ask how the task advances the team toward its key objectives? Keep this question perpetually in mind? Discontinue work that does not contribute to the mission?

- Show your commitment to the team through your level of work, standards, and willingness to help others improve their contributions?

- Step in to get the team back on track and focused on the bigger picture when the team becomes derailed? Push the team over humps on the way to achieving goals?

- Support fellow team members through their ups and downs? Help keep them motivated, putting their needs ahead of your own?

- Offer suggestions but support team decisions whether they go your way or not?

- Tackle tough team issues constructively? Ask: "Among our possible courses of action, which had the greatest potential for achieving key objectives fully and expeditiously?"

- Sacrifice your own time and energy and demonstrate accountability to achieve the most challenging objectives? Show determination? Go above and beyond to ensure the mission is fulfilled, especially when under pressure?

CORNERSTONE 3

GENERATING MOMENTUM

PROGRESS REQUIRES MOMENTUM

It's true in all fields of endeavor — business, community service, sports, military, and the arts, to mention a few. To borrow from Isaac Newton's first law of motion, a team remains stationary (or on its current trajectory) unless acted upon by a force — a force that produces greater velocity toward a goal. Catalysts are that force.

Momentum is defined in physics through a calculation of mass × velocity. For teams, mass might be viewed as its aggregate human talent with velocity created by how powerfully and efficiently those talents propel its strategy. Momentum is then reflected in the speed or tempo in which groups advance. It's evident in the group's energy, enthusiasm, persistence, and commitment. Yet creating the initial movement, significantly accelerating velocity, and picking up speed when climbing requires far more effort than to keep moving at the same rate. Just like riding a bike.

Catalysts build on team cohesiveness and use their credibility to generate momentum toward mission-relevant goals, build capacity to perform at ever higher levels, lead when best suited, and support the leadership of others.

> *You motivate by creating an environment in which individuals amplify their passion for a cause and embrace the value of achieving worthy objectives.*

INSPIRE TO VIGOROUSLY ACHIEVE LOFTY GOALS

Catalytic momentum mounts when individuals and groups aspire to fulfill a mission (purpose for being) and develop a vision of success. In essence, they ask themselves, if we are wildly successful, what will we achieve? They then direct their vigor, resources, and expertise in a common cause toward bringing it about. *You motivate by creating an environment in which individuals amplify their passion for a cause and embrace the value of achieving worthy objectives.* You ignite their energy. You create the environment in which they can choose to be passionate, motivated to achieve the goal, and to build momentum toward reaching it. But that is just how it begins; there is much more to creating a powerful force.

At sporting events, when a team is making a major comeback after falling behind in the game, momentum (mission-directed energy) can crescendo as the team closes the gap one play at a time. It's as if the momentum feeds on itself — generating more successive and powerful heads of steam — through the adrenaline it produces. Like in physics, with the dynamic between mass and velocity, a speeding object is hard to slow or stop.

Generating Momentum is the third of our catalytic cornerstones. Competencies for developing it include:

- Energizes Others to Execute with the Mission in Mind.

- Upgrades and Rejuvenates Skills and Knowledge.

- Leads and Follows.

7

ENERGIZES OTHERS TO EXECUTE WITH THE MISSION IN MIND

Definition: Ignites others to achieve organizational objectives.

Counter Behavior: Disengages from others. Saps organizational momentum. Expedient. Focuses on being busy rather than achieving key outcomes.

CYCLING AND ENERGIZING TOWARD A GOAL

Contrary to what casual observers may think, cycling is a team sport.

Although only one rider wins any given race or event segment, his or her victory is due to effective use of *team* tactics employed throughout the race. A cycling team fields a squad for a race and selects the rider on whom they are pinning their hopes for victory. The other six to eight riders work together to deploy several team tactics, including breakaway, drafting, lead-out train, and the peloton.

Breakaway

Early in a race stage, breakaways numbering two to five riders from multiple teams will attempt to separate themselves from the main field by pedaling hard for several miles. A rider making the breakaway is usually not the team's leader or may not be the strongest rider, but he strategically forces other teams to use energy or lose focus.

Drafting

As in auto racing, cyclists draft off each other to break the wind's resistance. A cycling team's director uses this race strategy, positioning the team's support riders, called *domestiques,* in front or to the side of the lead rider. This allows them to conserve from 20% to 40% of their energy throughout the race.

Lead-Out Train

Bike races that are on mostly flat terrain often end with a bunch sprint among specialists referred to as *sprinters.* They are able to accelerate quickly using powerful surges to sprint full speed to the finish line. The most successful cycling teams provide their sprinters with a well-rehearsed, lead-out train of three to four teammates sheltering the sprinter from the wind and clearing a path free of other riders. Timing within the lead-out train is essential as riders peel off one after another until, with 200–300 meters left, only the sprinter remains free to accelerate at full speed to the finish line.

Team Position within the Peloton

The main field of riders in a race, called a *peloton,* may have 180 cyclists in close quarters speeding along at 20–30 miles per hour. Therefore, a team director will likely have the riders spread throughout the peloton to ensure most survive a potential crash. Having riders sprinkled throughout the peloton will also allow the team director to cover or respond to attacks or break-aways when they occur.

TAKING ON THE SKYUKA MOUNTAIN

The roles of the domestiques are crucial, as mentioned earlier. They often ride in front of the team leader to enable him or her to draft, preserving substantial stores of energy for the lead rider when they need to breakout later in the race. In team attacks during the race, domestiques may surge ahead and force a rival team to lead a chase. As soon as the pack catches up, another domestique will surge ahead. The goal is to tire out the opposing teams and soften them up for a later run by the team leader.

One of the most accomplished domestiques in cycling is George Hincapie. Matt Tanner of Rollfast recounts a story in which George, as a friend and mentor, energized Matt to perform at a level he thought was impossible (personal communication, 2017). Matt and several others were out for a training ride, in this case an attack on Skyuka Mountain in South Carolina, which requires the cyclist to climb 550 meters over a 6.3 kilometer route. Professional riders describe the climb as brutal, painful, and quad-busting. Matt is in rare company finishing the climb in 25:37 minutes. He credits this level of performance to the encouragement of Hincapie.

George implored him to stay steady early in the climb, to not blow it up right away, but stay steady and keep energy reserves in the tank. The sprint to the top was brutal. Matt recounts his legs burning, lungs hurting, brain questioning, but he would not give up. Hincapie was there yelling into his ear, "only 200 meters further!" He was right there beside Matt; a physical presence at his side all the way. As Matt told us, "I would simply not give up; I could not give up. I would not disappoint someone who believed so strongly that I could do it. I would not disappoint myself. George's passion spurred me to reach into energy reserves that I did not realize existed." And as you might expect, it was several segments of "200 meters further" until he reached the top!

Matt's speed now ranks among the top 12 fastest times for this climb — to his great personal satisfaction. But his story is more about being energized by another rider than the accomplishment itself. From this experience, and others in his riding career, Matt knows the value of having someone on the team, in your corner, beside you on the bike who can boost and inspire you at crucial times. Catalysts, like George, make everyone on the team focus more sharply and dig deeper to perform just a bit better.

On Hincapie's part, he did several specific things that made a difference for Matt. He demonstrated the competency of energizes others by:

- Expressing his confidence in Matt's ability.

- Connecting with Matt on a personal level by getting to know him one-on-one.

- Staying with him all the way up the mountain, never leaving his side.

- Being "in his ear" in a positive, encouraging manner.

- Setting achievable goals.

- Breaking the ultimate goal into smaller chunks that seemed less daunting and more manageable.

- Motivating Matt to reach into himself to find more energy than he believed was possible.

- Celebrating the accomplishment with him.

To this day, Hincapie continues to reinforce and encourage Matt. How can you apply an energizing style like Hincapie's in your own way? How can you *energize* others or an entire team? How can you create velocity and sustain momentum that rises to catalytic levels?

Think about the cycling team and how they create ways for others to sprint forward. How can this happen in the teams that you are a part of? How can you pave the way for others? Putting team first is an essential part of this competency, part of which entails setting others up for success — and thereby achieving overall team success. Asking and strategizing with others to create the conditions for team success doesn't happen by accident. It wasn't by happenstance that riders created an opportunity for their teammates to draft — it was planned. How can you help others sprint forward, especially at crucial times?

> *From a functional perspective, effective team leaders are those who do, or who arrange to get done, whatever is critical for the team to accomplish its purpose.*
>
> — Walker, 2017

Catalysts energize mission-directed movement. It may be through their own hustle and calls to action, setting aggressive timelines that compel vigorous movement and task completion, and urging others to focus relentlessly on goals and the jobs that need to be finished to accomplish them. They set the example and put people in motion.

At the same time, catalysts are people-oriented. They harness individual motivations and talents, invigorate, and align collective efforts toward fulfilling a mission and realizing a vision. They ignite, guide, and fuel goal-directed action.

It does not happen magically. Understanding different types of people and what sparks their drive is a foundational ability. Some catalysts do it naturally, almost unconsciously. For others, it's a learned skill.

Sometimes people are described as either *results-oriented* or *relationship-oriented*. This phrasing assumes results, and that people are at opposite ends of a spectrum. It is a faulty characterization for how best to motivate others toward common goals. A catalytic leader realizes that both are integral to the overall equation: people are motivated in different ways and value a wide range of activities and ideas.

Psychologist David McClelland and his colleagues (McClelland, 1953) identified three significant motivational needs: need for achievement, need for affiliation, and need for power. These needs drive many aspects of human behavior. Generally speaking, all of us possess a mix of the three, yet one of these needs is usually stronger than the others, if not dominant. Effective catalysts are able to identify which is more important to a specific person. With this insight, they can determine effective ways of energizing or motivating others — and also identify meaningful outcomes or *wins* that will spur them on.

ENERGIZE TO ELEVATE PERFORMANCE

A cat chasing its tail wastes energy. There is no payoff, except perhaps fun from the fruitless exercise. That same energy directed toward catching its next meal has direct benefits, including the satisfaction of experiencing success. It's a well-honed skill that young felines in the wild learn by observing experienced cats, develop through trial and error, and perfect it based on what actually works for themselves and their pride.

For this competency, energy is produced when activity is externally directed — focused on goals, tangible accomplishments, and measurable outcomes. Energy is depleted if one denigrates others or instigates internal conflicts. Energy is also diverted by excessive contemplation or group introspection on issues that detract from the mission. These can be exhaustive undertakings that don't take the team anywhere or are certainly not worth the effort expended.

Generating and directing goal-oriented energy effectively entails working both smart and hard. Catalysts propel through positive actions by:

- Promoting pride, confidence, belief, and a robust unified team spirit.

- Identifying what's at stake.

- Making the mission and vision personally meaningful.

- Keeping the importance of the mission and its benefits uppermost in coworkers' minds.

- Conveying a "can-do" attitude and creating belief in what is possible.

- Reminding others regularly of personal and team rewards that will come with success.

Promote Pride, Confidence, Belief, and a Robust Unified Team Spirit

Team energy is generated primarily by its members and not by a magical external force — and catalysts accelerate its production. Necessary ingredients are a strong belief in the team's mission and what it stands for, pride in its purpose, confidence in the team's ability to succeed, and a spirit that unites members in their common undertaking. These are psychological dimensions that catalysts foster and use to override differences that might otherwise dampen performance. The spirit of teamwork depends on group members wholeheartedly supporting team decisions and direction, even when as individuals they may have advocated for a different path.

Identify What's at Stake

Catalysts articulate the positive consequences of success coupled with the downsides of falling short. A combination of the two can build greater determination, boost intensity, and energize the team's execution. They can be mobilizing forces. For some, the benefits of potential success are more motivational than the implications of failure. For others, it's the other way around. Catalysts strengthen the common cause while tapping into individual motivations.

Make the Mission and Vision Personally Meaningful

Catalysts advocate what's in it for each team member and for the greater good. They communicate repeatedly and in different ways the importance of the mission and vision and how fulfilling them will actualize individual and aggregate values.

Keep the Importance of the Mission and Its Benefits Uppermost in Coworkers' Minds

Using the team's overall purpose to invigorate and reinvigorate as necessary and repeating the same mantra frequently and genuinely can make it a powerful rallying cry.

Remind Others Regularly of the Personal Rewards and the Team's Rewards that Will Come with Success

These are personal and collective outcomes worth striving to attain, both tangible and intangible. Motivators should be personal — linked to what each team member aspires, which is also bound up in collective achievement. Integrate or fuse the "me" with the "we" for each stakeholder.

Convey a "Can-Do" Attitude. Catalysts Create Belief in What Is Possible

Remind the team how others have done it and that they have the where-withal to do it as well — in their own way. Catalysts accomplish this in a variety or ways.

They build on successes. Catalysts think of successes as milestones or stepping-stones for leaping to the next level. They celebrate triumphs and accomplishments and also identify lessons learned for going farther with greater effectiveness and speed. They extract the best practices and apply them going forward. They refuse to become bogged down by exercises that did not work.

They keep setbacks in perspective and use them as opportunities to learn. Catalysts often use setbacks as a way to rally the team to dig deep into its energy reserves and collective resourcefulness to pull the team back up — to achieve its way out of challenging circumstances — keeping its overarching objectives in mind. Encourage positive thinking. Help make the journey joyful and attainable in spite of misfortunes.

They work to actively foster a commitment to one another. Part of the glue that keeps a team together and performing at an energetic level is a commitment to each other. Catalysts recognize the interdependent relationships among team members and work to strengthen their mutual commitments. They understand that others rely on them and they, in turn, rely on others to achieve personal and team objectives. They instill the ethic of helping one another succeed, and in doing so, strengthen the entire team's ability to succeed. They build the case for not letting other team members down and avoiding lapses that impinge on another's productivity — and hence the team's performance and momentum. Like the peloton, they base their strategy on commitment to one another.

Finally, catalysts *empower others to innovate, develop, or discover novel solutions.* Goal-oriented empowerment, with accountability, generates energy, commitment, and ownership. Yet it's also important to recognize that empowered actions entail risks that may or may not pay off. Recognize and reinforce the effort and acceptable risk-taking, regardless of outcome. Identify lessons learned from what did and did not produce desired results. Then factor those findings into future activity. If you punish the failures, you then suppress future innovation and discourage initiative and empowered action. By positively recognizing and reinforcing innovative initiatives, you encourage more of it and produce more of the focused adrenaline that comes with it — as well as the possibility of leapfrogging forward. How can you encourage appropriate risk-taking and innovation and help the team learn from the resulting experience?

CHANNEL EXECUTION

Imagine a team of six horses pulling a stagecoach or wagon loaded with goods. Ideally, all the horses are aligned and pulling in the same direction. But what if they are not? What if they are tugging in slightly different directions, in essence fighting each other for the best way to go? The coach or wagon will jerk back and forth based on the different directional tugs. This conflict wastes energy and muscle that could be pulling together in a straight row. It's inefficient and makes the ride far rougher than necessary. This is analogous to what happens on many human teams. Although the members are not harnessed together, they may be moving in slightly (or not so slightly) different directions based on their own inclinations, rather than in an aligned and coordinated fashion. As a result, there is greater conflict, less effectiveness, and squandered talent or human resources — and the team takes longer to get where it needs to go while expending excessive energy. Catalysts act to create a dynamic and unified spirit, retain alignment, and facilitate synchronized team action to heighten efficient productivity. They work and channel their credibility and influence to energize the team through the following eight techniques.

Connect Individual and Team Goals with the Team's Mission and Vision

Catalysts define the explicit interrelated roles and accountabilities of each contributor and how collective goal-driven individual execution, in concert with others, drives the team closer to its big picture objectives.

In Google's early days, when it had only 40 employees, they applied a process designed by John Doerr, a venture capitalist, to focus and drive performance. It was called OKRs for Objectives and Key Results. Numerous high-tech firms, other companies large and small, and many non-profit organizations including the Gates Foundation now use OKR. With OKR, individual objectives are based on the organization's mission; key results define specific measurable interim steps and concrete milestones on the path toward achieving the objectives. The results also describe how the objectives are reached and what represents progress.

Catalytic leaders continually assess their own performance and how well it promotes fulfilling the firm's mission. They commit to achieving OKR first by recording them on paper, keeping them visible, acting on them, and bringing them to mind as they begin each task or project. In the process, they may "chunk" key results into smaller increments (or sub-mileposts to keep interval distances short) to retain focus, stay motivated, and ensure they are moving in the right direction. Catalytic leaders and team members are accountable to themselves as well as others.

Identify Team Milestones. Chart Progress

The OKR process was designed for individuals, but its methods may be used to establish team OKR as well. The steps in using OKR in a team setting might be to:

1. Realistically map out how far and how fast the group can go given its resources. Identify logical mileposts (key results or interim accomplishments on the path).

2. Describe in concrete terms how the team will know when it has reached each one. Use the milestones, when reached, as opportunities to assess progress, adjust processes, and make mid-course corrections as needed.

Retain Focus on the Mission: Stop, Start, Continue

Catalysts continually ask:

- How is what we are doing getting us closer to our goals?

- How well does each activity contribute toward fulfilling our mission?

These questions will help determine when to discontinue or phase out activities that are not moving the team forward or rapidly enough, activities that take it offtrack, or tasks that are disconnected to its overall purpose. These are diversions that siphon resources from more relevant and productive mission-driven work. Ask:

- Are we wasting time and energy in some instances? If so, how can we redirect energy that is not paying off to move us ahead faster?

- Are there individuals working on projects or tasks that are not highly valued-adding? If so, how can we redeploy them more effectively?

- Which activities are consuming or draining? Which are taking more energy, time, money, and other resources than the value they yield?

- Conversely, which activities are really paying off for us? Which are contributing substantially toward achieving our mission? These are the obvious activities you want to continue, strengthen, or expand — since they are generating results.

Simply stated, these questions will help you and your team decide what to *Stop*, what to *Start*, and what to *Continue* in order to accelerate progress and generate the highest potential payoff. Make your Stop, Start, Continue list and update it frequently with your team.

Pursue a Synchronized Course of Action to Achieve Specific Outcomes

Synchronization reduces resistance. Less resistance leads to smoother execution and greater ability to build one success on top of another in the drive toward overarching goals. In this regard, healthy relationships, chemistry, and communication among team members are crucial. Role clarity and clear lines of sight to strategic outcomes help align collective efforts. They also define how the group as a whole should operate for seamless execution and to fluidly develop team momentum.

Advocate for Taking Advantage of the Best Expertise on the Team for a Given Challenge

A growing body of research cited by Rob Cross and associates in "Managing Collaboration at the Point of Execution" (Cross et al., 2008) dispels the common notion that team consensus is crucial. They have found that, contrary to popular thought, applying the most relevant expertise on the team is more effective than a "heavy emphasis on consensus and participative leadership." (Cross et al., 2008) Their research reveals that "excessive consensus building" often slows decision-making and therefore execution. The challenge for catalysts, then, is to influence the team's trajectory by emphasizing the pertinent expertise of others rather than pushing for team concurrence or majority rule. The latter may make members feel more involved but may at times undermine the team's effectiveness in executing its mission, especially for key challenges or at critical points. The objective should be to tap the most qualified expertise for addressing a specific challenge or need, which yields better team results than consensus itself.

Catalytic leaders possess courage and "a network view" (Cross et al., 2008) that allow them to offer insights and access well-aimed ideas that keep the team from becoming too dependent on members who tend to be the most vocal. They are adept at facilitating these other tactical experts into supportive followers for the purpose at hand. While the most knowledgeable and expert voices can be pivotal — and reflect experience and wisdom that is probably foolish to ignore — it's also important to appropriately allow others to apply their knowledge and expertise to help refine the ideas. Get their fingerprints on the emerging plan to build their commitment to it. There is usually not just one *right solution* but multiple ways to accomplish goals. Seek and embrace ideas that refine or strengthen the core approach recommended by those with the greatest relevant expertise.

You do not need to view consensus as 100% agreement on all the details by everyone in the room. That is difficult, if not impossible to achieve in most situations. We recommend that you approach consensus in your team by defining it as more than 80% agreement with the decisions we have made and 100% commitment to implementing them.

The latter 100% commitment is key. Team members ideally will leave the room, the floor, or the stage with the feeling that "even though I did not completely agree with every detail, I am fully committed to achieving what we have decided to accomplish together. And, I will publicly support our team decisions (and not undermine them with snarky comments in the hallway)."

Influence Discussions That Take Place Outside of Formal Meetings to Keep Teams Focused and On Course with the Mission and Vision

Often, loud power-seeking voices try to sway activity away from a team's formally determined path (Cross et al., 2008). It's these conversations that may disrupt, sow discord and doubt, and derail strategies — somewhat like the stagecoach horses tugging in different directions. Catalytic leaders and team members maintain alignment and coordinated action. When necessary, they redirect tactics and strategies back on overarching objectives and plans.

Seek Fresh Perspectives on How to Invigorate, Improve, and Direct Team Performance

Teams and organizations benefit from outside and new perspectives to discover alternative ways of meeting challenges. Catalysts develop high-quality relationships built on trust and candor. They use what they learn to improve how their team navigates and to propel it forward with greater energy and effectiveness. They seek to understand how customers and stakeholders perceive the team and how it can improve. Keep in mind, a team's success is linked to how well it contributes to its internal and external customers' success.

Keep the Team on Track

Prevent the team from getting detoured by minor details that can derail or dilute its focus. If it does, serve as its compass to guide the team back on course. Keep it aligned with overarching goals, its overall purpose or mission, and its aim on realizing the vision — what the team aspires to become or create.

Make the mission a magnet.

CONCLUSION

There is no one way to energize others to execute with the mission in mind. Individual and team velocity may be generated through a combination of techniques and strategies. The key is to efficiently direct talents and energy toward accomplishing overarching goals and key results integral to reaching them. It's also important not to mistake activity for results-directed performance. Like the cat chasing its tail, it's easy to unintentionally go around in circles or to spend excess time on low-value activities, which may be interesting but don't create momentum. Velocity is developed through actions that inspire the team to vigorously achieve lofty goals, elevate individual and team performance, and channel execution onto clear paths for achieving mission-relevant outcomes.

Take a moment to reflect on your own behavior, do you:

- Understand your organization's mission clearly and are able to articulate it to others with energy and passion?

- Behave in a way that leads to fulfillment of the mission?

- Remove obstacles that distract from the results orientation of the team as a whole?

- Help others remove obstacles that may be in their way?

- Check each team member's commitment to the team's goals? Embrace that the results are not just your results — they are the team's results?

- Use the Stop, Start, Continue framework to examine your activities?

- Seek a reasonable approach to building consensus that moves the team forward?

- Drive momentum to inspire the team to vigorously achieve lofty goals?

8

UPGRADES AND REJUVENATES SKILLS AND KNOWLEDGE

Definition: Seeks and acquires leading-edge knowledge and expertise. Curious about new developments and concepts and how to apply them.

Counter Behaviors: Content with current skill and knowledge set. Rebuffs suggestions and opportunities for improvement.

REVITALIZING AN INNER-CITY SCHOOL: THE PROCESS THAT CREATED A COMMUNITY OF CATALYSTS

The new principal of an urban middle school swung into action.

She outlined her key objectives during the first meeting with faculty and staff: to significantly "improve student achievement and create a socially equitable, developmentally responsive" learning environment (Thompson & McKelvy, 2007). The centerpiece of the strategy involved transforming the school into a professional learning community using Peter Senge's five disciplines (2006) as a roadmap for improvement. The principal saw them as key to revitalizing the school and making it a place where teachers were truly "committed to their students' intellectual, emotional, and social growth." (Thompson & McKelvy, 2007)

Right from the start, she inspired the faculty and all of the staff to *dream big*. She persuaded them to think expansively and view the school as an educational enterprise — to see it as a whole, how it all worked together as a *system* — and not just from the perspective of their individual departments or functions.

Following Senge's model, their first goal was to *develop a shared vision* —
what did they want the school to look like and be in five years? The principal placed this among her highest priorities and considered it key to creating
a sense of community among staff, parents, students, and other stakeholders.
This shared vision would drive all their decisions. To develop it, they talked
extensively about what students needed to know and be able to do after
graduation. The outcomes of those visioning discussions, along with an
assessment of student needs, determined what the staff needed to know and
do to generate desired student growth and achievement. The skills and
knowledge they concentrated on fell into five "strands:" depth of knowledge,
technology, diversity, pedagogy (age-appropriate teaching practices), and
learning theory. Teachers also made commitments to further develop their
own mastery.

Based on their shared vision and analyses, a series of key decisions were
made that fundamentally changed many school practices:

- The school day was reorganized to allow interdisciplinary and subject
  matter teams to plan together.

- Faculty study groups were formed that focused on professional development and performance improvement.

- Arrangements were made with a university to help teachers deepen their
  subject knowledge.

- Programs and activities that did not align with the vision were discontin-
  ued. New initiatives that aligned with the new vision were launched, and
  the staff learned how to deliver them.

In keeping with Peter Senge's five disciplines (2006), existing mental
models were critically examined, adjusted, or rescinded. New mental models
were developed to more effectively accomplish student learning and achieving objectives. Teacher, student, parent, and support staff leaders were
invited to participate in the process, making it inclusive and ensuring it
reflected the range of perspectives. The purpose was to make the endeavor a
community-wide effort; instill commitment, ownership, and pride; and
develop leaders in all areas. Everyone was expected to embrace the new
approaches and fulfill their roles in implementing them.

It wasn't just students that needed to learn and grow differently.
Consistent with Senge's five disciplines (2006), a driving idea was that all

stakeholders in the school community should actively learn and grow to help advance toward the vision and achieve objectives. With this in mind, the school staff prepared professional development plans based on their individual needs.

Another key component of the school's strategy entailed taking *team learning* to a new level. They moved beyond the traditional interdisciplinary and departmental teams to create what we call *catalytic leaders and team members*. They helped each other to personally and professionally grow, break new ground, challenge thinking, and stimulate progress throughout the school.

They began to meet on a rotating basis in each other's classrooms. Their first and most important agenda item was always to assess each classroom's learning environment and offer feedback and ideas to enhance it. They ensured each classroom was designed to support key student-learning objectives. They shared ideas and information that addressed the full scope of the *learning environment and system*. They designed thematic learning plans together along with assessments to measure progress. They helped each other solve problems. They asked each other to observe how they delivered new or challenging lessons, and offered feedback and suggestions for improvement.

Whether you are age two or ninety-two, the work of learning is never done.

The culture of this urban middle school was completely transformed. Teachers didn't just teach, they ignited the curiosity of their students. As learning models for students, the teachers *mastered new skills*, shared what they learned, and many became catalysts that contributed meaningfully to elevating the school's performance. Today, they work in concert to successfully live out the school's mission: "... to build relationships to support student success for learning and teach students to apply the knowledge and utilize the skills that are instilled in them daily, to be ready and 'prepared' for life." (Thompson & McKelvy, 2007)

CREATING A COMMUNITY OF CATALYSTS

Instead of thinking about the middle school as an institution and a corporation as a monolith, think of them as networks comprising many teams, each with their own purpose and objectives that align with the overarching organizational strategy. One way catalytic leaders and members enable their teams to outperform others is to employ Senge's five practices (2006) as vital to the development of learning organizations. In various combinations, they produce a catalytic effect. Let's take a closer look at Senge's five practices (2006).

1. Systems thinking: Catalysts promote systems thinking (seeing the big picture and seeing how all the pieces fit together) for analyzing situations, innovating, and problem-solving. Senge considers this discipline, along with a shared vision, as fundamental because the other disciplines are woven into them.

2. Building a shared vision: Catalysts cultivate a shared vision or aspiration with stakeholders inside and outside of their group.

3. Personal mastery: Catalysts continuously develop greater proficiency in areas key to improving their personal performance. They are application-oriented and encourage others to achieve greater mastery and excellence.

4. Mental models: Catalysts identify mental models (perspectives for examining circumstances and decision-making) and they challenge potentially faulty assumptions. They also address models that impede communication and learning for themselves and others. They strive to open communication channels and facilitate flexible and fluid thinking.

5. Team learning: Catalysts stimulate learning and team building to improve the group's ability to work together effectively and efficiently, as well as achieve goals as a synergistic unit.

These five disciplines promote collaborative learning and the continual upgrading and rejuvenation of skills and knowledge. This is what Senge refers to as learning organizations — places "where people continually expand their capacity to create the results they truly desire, where new and expansive patterns of thinking are nurtured, where collective aspiration is set free, and where people are continually learning to see the whole together." (2006, p. 3)

Does the application and integration of Senge's five disciplines (2006) produce catalytic results? Research conducted by Bersin for Deloitte (Bersin, 2012) revealed that performance-oriented learning organizations "delivered profit growth three-times greater than their competitors" over a four-year period. His research also showed that learning organizations have shifted from a "pure focus on 'training programs' to a focus on 'organizational capability development.'" These capabilities — the collective skills, abilities, and expertise of an organization — are the outcome of investments in staffing, training, compensation, communication, and other human resources areas. They represent the ways that people and resources are brought together to accomplish work (Smallwood & Ulrich, 2004). This makes skill development an essential and critical activity for learning at all three levels: individual, team, and organizational.

Catalysts see learning as continuous.

UPGRADING AND REJUVENATING OUR OWN SKILLS

Many of us think of learning experiences as discrete events, such as a training seminar or skill development workshop. But training, while an important contributor to continual professional development, does not strengthen workplace performance by itself. The subsequent, disciplined application of learned skills and knowledge is what results in new behaviors sticking in ways that contribute to catalytic behavior.

Catalysts see learning as continuous; as occurring through everyday experiences that cumulatively heighten their effectiveness and efficiency, as well as their influence on the performance of their teams and others — teammates, coworkers, and other stakeholders. In addition to training seminars or workshops, there are other activities that will engrain new learnings into your behavior. Below are several approaches to consider.

Practice — and More Practice

Practice is crucial to strengthening skills and retaining knowledge. One of the most well-known studies on this topic was originally published in 1885 (and later translated into English in 1913) by Hermann Ebbinghaus (1913) and it has been replicated in various forms many times since (Murre, & Dros, J., 2015). In essence, the research demonstrates that without review or practice, whatever is retained at the end of a learning session, often about

75%, will fall to 30% 15 hours later and between 3% and 21%, 30 days later. Applications and practices are crucial to retention and developing greater expertise.

Experimentation

Experimenting will allow you to seek new ways to achieve goals more effectively: develop, explore, and refine innovations through trial and error — and extract lessons learned. Fail forward. Pass on learning points to others. Rinse and repeat.

Curiosity

Knowledge and insights can be acquired through the simple acts of asking questions, seeking to learn more, inquiring how others may see or analyze matters differently, and understanding their logic. So be *curious*. Tobi Lütke, the chief executive of Shopify, described his thirst for learning during an interview with Adam Bryant for the Corner Office column in *The New York Times* (2016). He reflected that going back to his elementary school days, he has had "a weird obsession with optimizing things." (cited in Bryant, 2016) Regarding his work, he said, "I'm always trying to think of ways to make something more efficient." (cited in Bryant, 2016) In describing the team that helped him start Shopify he explained, "We are all super committed learners, ferocious readers, and personal-growth junkies. So we really committed to giving each other feedback, and we're trying to expand that to the entire company." (cited in Bryant, 2016) That is *curiosity on steroids*, which has helped make his executive team and company a leader in the industry.

Ways to Learn

- Seeking out others — These may include coaches and mentors, peers, teammates, coworkers, colleagues in other organizations, and friends. Proactively seek what makes them effective, what can be learned from them and their experience, and draw out applied lessons for yourself.

- Self-learning through reading, videos, Internet searches. Do you constantly seek state-of-the-art information? Be the self-learning guru of your team.

- Shadowing others. Catalytic leaders and teammates should understand the needs and challenges of their coworkers, both inside and outside their functional area, so they know how best to support others and be an asset that elevates performance or creates value for others. This may be as an internal supplier or customer. Think of these as apprenticeships for the experienced employee: you can walk a mile in a teammate's shoes. Act like an internal entrepreneur who wants to become increasingly indispensable by understanding others' roles in depth.

- Benchmarking and adapting best practices. Identify the best at your position outside of your team or outside of your industry or area. Find out why they are as good as they are and how you can adapt or incorporate their techniques to enhance your own performance.

- Structured educational experiences. Explore online, blended, classroom, professional seminars and workshops to enhance, widen, and deepen what you know and how to apply it effectively. Catalysts focus on application and elevating performance.

TEAM AND ORGANIZATIONAL LEARNING

Beyond what we do as individuals are the endeavors of an entire team, group, or organization. They are also charged with upgrading and rejuvenating collective skill sets in order to become more successful as working units. Leading, driving, and ultimately succeeding in those efforts is an ongoing process — and a continual challenge, even after such cultural expectations are well embedded.

As Casey Stengel, when he was manager of the New York Yankees and guiding the team to seven World Series titles, said, "Getting good players is easy, gettin 'em to play together is the hard part." (cited in Popik, 2012)

We recommend supplementing workshops and team-building exercises with an array of other learning activities, since research shows training sessions have only a moderate impact on actual team performance (Salas, Rozell, Mullen, & Driskell, 1999), and when it does, it's usually on processes and affective outcomes (Salas et al., 2008) rather than tangible results. Bringing about enduring group behavioral change is a formidable undertaking and is usually best achieved through a range of learning interventions. Think of training workshops as great kick-off events that can get the ball rolling, create a common platform for change, and through subsequent sessions reinforce or improve practices — but they are not necessarily sufficient in and of themselves. They can be entertaining, but do they add value to your team and its work?

It is the implementation of learning back at work that makes it stick, leads to effective adaptations and extensions, and creates momentum to improve. To improve team skills and knowledge, incorporate the eight practices in the following sections into your team's regimen.

> *I see it in myself. When I fall into not practicing, I quickly find myself getting unhappy, because I am not adhering to my own professional standards — I rot from the inside out. That's the biggest thing — true musicians always want to change and grow. They are people who are well prepared and have energy — I thrive by being around them.*
>
> — Concert master of a major symphony orchestra
> (personal communication, 2010)

Practice Together

Project teams, crews, ensembles, orchestras, and troupes practice even when they are excellent at what they do. They do not take proficiency or success for granted. Olympic athletes and master musicians know this from experience. They recognize the value of practicing both individually and together to strengthen their collective performance — to ensure they are supporting each other, coordinating well, operating like a well-oiled machine, achieving goals, and elevating their overall performance.

Businesswoman Farnoosh Brock, founder of PROLIFIC*living*, eloquently makes the point, "When you practice, you use your skills and you build on them. You start to break boundaries, the ones you swore you'd never be able to do; you push past your old edge and start playing around new ones. Simply put, you get better with practice." (n.d.) Later in the same post Brock (n.d.) writes, "Consistent and regular practice has more of an exponential than a linear effect. If you practice daily, the jump is not linear. It is exponential — in other words, it's a big jump, a huge jump, the kind of jump that makes the difference between good and great, mediocre and magnificent."

Debriefing Sessions

Debriefing sessions entail critically examining what did and did not go well and how to improve in the future. For example, although they are the world's best leaders of the Israeli emergency medical teams, the Israel Defense Forces evaluate how their teams performed after every disaster relief operation. They seek ways to fix or prevent problems and how to get better, faster, more efficient, and more effective for the next one, wherever it may be (Leichman, 2016).

Team Problem-Solving

Great teams solve problems when they are first identified and usually when they are small or beginning to germinate. Problems usually do not go away by themselves. The key is to learn from them and use them as a platform for getting better. Some key steps include: identifying/defining the problem (using data when possible), analyzing the problem, determining what a solution should do, and generating and evaluating potential solutions through a dedicated process (Polya, 1973).

Guiding and Assisting Each Other

Catalytic teams are not created — they are built. You can drive the search for learning that your team needs. Look beyond your job to help others grow. Keep your head up. Help each individual perform better. Your team's performance will benefit.

Experimentation

Of course we learn from what works, what we are positively reinforced to repeat. But sometimes learning what does not work, from missteps or failures, is just as valuable. Research by McKinsey & Company revealed, "Managers and employees broadly agree about the attitudes, values, and behavior that promote innovation. Topping the list ... were openness to new ideas and a willingness to experiment and take risks. In an innovative culture, employees know that their ideas are valued and believe that it is safe to express and act on those ideas and to learn from failure." (Barsh, Capozzi, & Davidson, 2008) Experiments can help you discover how to improve and apply new information and develop existing skill sets.

Benchmarking and Team Best Practices

At the organizational or team level, identify the techniques that high-performing teams or organizations employ that can be adapted for your team's purpose and objectives. Do not limit your search for best practices to your own industry or field. In their early years, Southwest Airlines conducted a famous benchmarking study that was designed to uncover practices for improving team performance (Ghete, 2004). The company's objective was to significantly reduce aircraft turnaround time from when planes arrived at the airport gates to when they are pushed back for departure. Faster turnarounds meant more planes in the air, increased income, and more customers getting to their destinations on time. In addition to studying other airlines, they also benchmarked the best practices of NASCAR pit crews. Pit crews must change the tires, refuel the car, clean the grill, check the radiator, make mechanical adjustments, and fix anything that is not working properly in seconds (NASCAR.com, 2015). The roles are highly specialized, as are the functions that must be performed when turning planes around — from cabin cleaning, and unloading and loading baggage, to helping travelers with special needs. Southwest continues its exemplary turnaround performance as witnessed at the Denver International Airport. At a typical hub, planes may be on the ground for 90 minutes. Southwest has "... six flights arrive at exactly the same time, and all leave 35 minutes later," Dave LaPorte, the airline's station manager in Denver told *The Denver Post* (Leib, 2010).

LEARNING AT THE ORGANIZATIONAL, TEAM, AND INDIVIDUAL LEVELS: A FAMILIAR SETTING

The McDonald's brothers cast a vision of *fast-food* restaurants that has transformed the industry to this day. We observed this modern-day impact up close during our interviews with crewmembers. What or who drove the original transformation of this system? Two brothers with good ideas and a willingness to learn.

In the film *The Founder* (Handfield, Lunder, Renner, Ryder, (Producers) & Hancock, (Director), 2016), the McDonald's, "Mac" and Dick, took their crewmembers to a tennis court and marked off the areas of the restaurant's kitchen in chalk. The dimensions of a McDonald's kitchen are the same as a tennis court down to a couple of inches. On the court, they orchestrated the movement of the crew from preparation to cooking to packaging and delivery; each movement was examined relative to speed and efficiency and adjusted accordingly. The excitement and energy were palpable among the team members involved. A new set of movements was being learned by the individual crewmembers; the teams worked together in new ways, the process was transformed, increased efficiency and speed of the system were possible!

Thomas C. Dolly describes the scene: "Sweeping in from the Mojave, the brisk autumn wind carried an invigorating bite, hinting at an unseasonable winter squall. It was late, and little past 11:00 p.m. Seven men strode onto a well-lit tennis court located behind a stately, white-columned southern style mansion. Two men consulted over a sheet of paper and spoke in firm positive tones as they supervised the activities of the other five. Red chalk perimeter lines and carefully composed geometric shapes were drawn and redrawn on the court's smooth surface.

When the rendering was complete, the men carefully arranged themselves at various locations in relation to the lines and shapes. Gesturing and speaking as they passed, the men moved from place to place, pausing and stopping, first before one shape then another. The allemande continued — right then left, again and again — past midnight into the predawn chill. Finally, at 2:00 a.m., the men were satisfied and dispersed. A curious neighbor may well have mistaken these nocturnal antics as some sort of giant outdoor board game — or perhaps a fraternal group rehearsing a holiday square dance routine. The drawing was, in fact, a full-scale floor plan and equipment layout for McDonald's new self-service concept. The supervisors were Mac and Dick McDonald!" ("Pure Americana: The Founding of McDonald's," http://jpatton.bellevue.edu/micro/mcdonalds.html).

This scene captures the intense curiosity that the brothers brought to their work and their team. Seeking to build a new way of delivering food quickly was their vision and passion. By adjusting the way they viewed their facility and how it worked, they were able to experiment with new concepts and how to apply them successfully. As you may know, the business side of the venture did not end as well as desired for the McDonald brothers: Ray was accused of not living up to their business agreements.

But the passion for learning about new ways to operate that was displayed by the brothers, along with Ray, provided the impetus for growth in McDonald's stores that now dot the landscapes and satisfy the palates of people around the world.

CONCLUSION

Catalytic leaders are lifelong learners and focus on how they can apply what they learn to improve performance for themselves, others, and their teams. They focus on learning in multiple ways and embed learning opportunities in their daily work habits.

If you are innately curious about things, you may find that you are frequently the one asking the most questions and sparking discussion. If you are passionate about development opportunities, you are often the one pushing the limits on your organization's education programs. You may be the team member who is watching more game film to analyze and adjust to the opposing team's tendencies. Accomplished musicians attend master classes to enhance their contributions and achieve higher levels of excellence.

You've seen from the story above, and our interviews with crewmembers at a McDonald's restaurant, that the company continues to foster individual and team growth in order to improve. In the case of the high-performing store we studied, the owner/manager was an inspirational mentor and supporter of her employees, continually talking with them one-on-one about how they can improve, taking personal interest in their growth, and reinforcing how much they impact the success of the team and the store.

Underlying the activities for continuous team learning and skill improvement must be a common commitment to goals, the team's approach, and overall purpose (De Meuse, 2009). Upgrading and rejuvenating skills and knowledge must be an ongoing process. Continual catalytic performance depends on it. As good as you may be as an individual performer, you can always get better. So can teams. It's a matter of committing to learning processes that support all 12 competencies identified in the Catalyst Effect and setting clear goals for improvement for each individual and the team.

Take a moment to reflect on your own behavior, do you:

- Spark a sense of urgency to improve performance in order to keep pace with competitors?

- Identify clear and measurable team and organizational goals for improvement?

- Identify and convey the skills and behaviors new people should possess or develop; check to ensure sure everyone knows their own personal improvement goals?

- Rally key influencers to help lead the learning process by example?

- Recognize progress regularly; reinforce new behaviors?

- Take advantage of every education reimbursement dollar your employer offers? Bring what you've learned back to the team?

- Propose an "on-the-job" sabbatical to learn a new skill or dedicate time to shadow another individual from whom you can learn?

- Stretch? Ask your boss, mentor, or coach, "What do you think I need to do to be outstanding?"

9

LEADS AND FOLLOWS

Definition: Leads when best qualified to accelerate progress toward objectives. Partners with others or follows the leadership of others when their knowledge and expertise are well suited to the task. Demonstrates respect for the abilities of others.

Counter Behaviors: Insists on doing things own way and knows what is best. Considers self to be indispensable. May undermine others.

LEAD... FOLLOW... LEAD... FOLLOW...

Improv is a microcosm of leading and following. It breaks down the behavior into discrete units of give and take, encouraging players to take the lead for a while and then step back to follow. This idea also plays out in teams and organizations, whether in business, sports, or the arts. Improv requires that players in a skit are fully in sync — that they move naturally and interact positively and creatively at all times. It requires most of all that participants or actors *know when to lead and when to follow.*

We had the opportunity in our interviews to gain fresh insights into the dynamics of improv from an amateur player. Beth is the senior member of a group of young adults that meets each month to explore their ability to work spontaneously with each other to create a story, in real time, and share it on stage. By day, she is a highly regarded executive at a symphony orchestra; in the evenings, she can often be found playing with her improv friends.

She commented:

Senior member means I'm a 40-something playing on stage with 20- and 30-somethings. I love it! I learn... I share... I follow... I lead. And I'm steadily getting better at going with the flow! Improv has stretched me immensely. By taking risks with these folks, I've learned a ton about myself as a team member, a teacher, and a manager. It definitely helps build my confidence in up front situations at work.

By way of background, I'm a late bloomer when it comes to improv. I'm the oldest person in our group but by no means am I the most talented. I'm a work in progress when it comes to being on stage. A grade school experience set the foundation for me being interested in the arts, music, and acting. I was terribly shy as a young girl. If there was a quiet wallflower in the classroom it was me. I was NOT the person who was outgoing or noticed.

Then something extraordinary occurred. A new girl moved into town and joined my class mid-year. We became fast friends and as we got to know each other we decided that, hey, we liked being together, but we also wanted to have more friends! But we didn't know how to go about this. There was not a course in 4th grade about how to overcome shyness and make friends!

I was certainly too shy to approach other kids and engage them in a way that would build some type of relationship. If it was up to me alone, it was simply not going to happen. But my new (and only) friend, Sarah, suggested that we pretend — that we play 'as if' we were extraverted young girls and not shy at all. And guess what? It worked!

In a strange way, that was the beginning of my interest in the arts, the inception of my improv stage career and my ability and confidence to now build relationships everywhere I go.

Improv is almost exactly like my role-playing as a young girl. It demands that I place myself in a situation in a moment's notice and build relationships with my fellow players for a few minutes of intense interaction. We must know when to take the lead...and when to follow the other person or people in the skit.

There is no time for self-doubt. It is not constructive to criticize and say 'no' or 'but' to the ideas of others. Rather, improv is about the power of 'and!' It is about embracing an idea that someone brings to the group and trusting each other to explore it to its fullest and most creative limits. (personal communication, 2016)

Having a successful experience on stage for Beth and her fellow players, as well as for the audience, requires that they do not negate others' ideas — but affirm and build on them instead. It is about the inviting power of "and".... not the negatives experienced in "but."

It also requires that the scenes in the skit move seamlessly from moment to moment around a particular topic or theme. It is a verbal dance: one person takes the lead and sets the scene with an introductory invitation; the other person, or people, follow(s) that lead and respond. At a moment's notice, the person who was leading the dialogue becomes the responder or the follower. Extensions of the themes are sparked and explored; energy abounds. Through the give and take, leading and then following, they build off each other's ideas, they fully engage with each other, and delight the audience.

LEADING, PARTNERING, AND FOLLOWING

People often think of leading and following as opposite ends of a spectrum. In some circumstances, you may be the best person to lead based on your experience, skills, and knowledge. In other situations, someone else may have stronger or deeper capabilities for advancing the team toward specific objectives, even when you have assumed leadership responsibilities. Being able to make those judgment calls well is a sign of catalytic leadership, not weakness. Yet there is a middle point in the spectrum which entails shared responsibility and accountability: that is, partnership.

Sometimes it's the pooling of different individual strengths that's the most effective leadership course. Catalysts forge these partnerships or commit to following based on the best interests of the team and assessments of how to best achieve key objectives. One need not abdicate leadership to work in tandem with another or to allow someone else to take the lead at times and to then follow.

Following is not a passive activity. It's not gliding. It's striving as part of the team and supporting whoever is in the lead. It's contributing in many forms through work, dedication, expertise, ideas, promoting unity, and collaborating to determine the best path forward.

Great leaders have also been partners and followers. They are committed to doing whatever it takes to fulfill the mission and using the strengths of other team members to accomplish goals. What's important to them is impact, getting results through the best means possible. Credit, recognition, and power, if important to them at all, are secondary.

Consider for a moment an astronaut crew in space, which has parallels to teamwork on Earth. When something goes wrong or there is an in-flight crisis, unexpected issue, or when a significant miscalculation jeopardizes their flight trajectory, they can't stop flying. They must keep going while they fix the problem, usually in collaboration with the ground operation. The commander must make decisions under pressure and draw on the expertise of other crewmembers. Each has specialized skills. It doesn't matter who is the designated leader. What matters is who has the greatest ability to correct the problem so the crew can complete its journey safely. That astronaut becomes the leader for that need. The commander's task is to empower, partner, support, and follow, to help the specialist succeed.

It's no different than a cross-functional or project team with an assignment to complete, a client services team, a cyber security team, a special operations unit, surgical team in the midst of an operation, firefighting company, or any other team with a mission to complete. A catalyst passes the leadership baton when that's the best way forward.

The story of British explorer Ernest Shackleton's leadership during his third Antarctic expedition, from 1914 to 1917, is a case in point (Wharton@Work, Executive Education, Leadership, 2012). His ship, *Endurance*, sank after sailing into and being crushed by pack ice. Stranded on the ice, he relied on the resourcefulness and specialized expertise of crewmembers and allowed them to take the lead so they could all get back safely. His carpenter led the construction of a boat that could carry them all while capable of withstanding over 720 miles of rough stormy seas. Shackleton also gave his navigator the lead at times during the hazardous open-sea journey to ensure they maintained their course to Elephant Island. He knew when the expertise of others was crucial and the best way forward.

Sometimes the movement from leader to follower or partner is fluid and natural. It may come from a history of working together and trusting one another. At other times, it may be more discrete or done by necessity. Catalysts make these judgments and act based on their own leadership style.

Judgment Factors when Deciding Whether to Transfer Leadership or Partner

- Does the task or endeavor play to my strengths or does someone else have stronger skills and greater knowledge for leading it?

- Does the other person have the credibility to lead?

- What should be the parameters of leadership passed to others? Should you be transferring leadership of all or part of the endeavor or continue leading certain parts?

- Who will have overall accountability?

- How can I best support the other person?

Effective followership practices:

- Dedicate yourself to helping the task leader and team succeed. Do what it takes to help the team achieve its objectives. Remain results-oriented.

- Encourage cooperation, collaboration, and teamwork.

- Promote team unity.

- Solve problems.

- Work as hard as you would if you were the leader. Fulfill your obligations.

- Step up as needed.

- Let the leader and the team know that he or she has your support and confidence.

- Encourage other team members.

- Communicate effectively and honestly with the leader.

- Do not undermine. Address concerns and issues in a constructive, supportive, and forthright way — which may be done privately, rather than in front of others.

- Do what is best for the team and its mission.

- Continue to be an independent thinker.

- Help build consensus when needed.

Effective partnership practices, in addition to all of the above:

- Define what success looks like together — including goals and metrics.

- Establish role clarity. Define each other's role and the parameters.

- Agree on how you will work together, collaborate, solve problems, and handle issues; support each other; and communicate with the rest of the team.

- Create structure and protocols as needed.

- Identify potential barriers, from the beginning, and how you will overcome them together.

- Assess problems and agree on an approach for addressing them. Brainstorm solutions.

- Acknowledge mistakes. Help each other correct them. Avoid blaming each other.

- Be open to each other's ideas.

- Review together the strengths and weaknesses of team members and decide how best to deploy available talent and how to supplement as needed.

- Be flexible. Adjust your roles as needed to improve your working relationship and accelerate progress.

- Give each other positive and constructive feedback. Discuss how to help each other improve.

THE ART OF FOLLOWING

In all likelihood, virtually everyone reading this book has something in common: you are each in situations when you need to follow others.

If you are an NBA coach, you answer to a general manager. If you are the CEO of a Fortune 500 firm, you answer to a board of directors. If you are the head rabbi of a large synagogue, you answer to a board of trustees... and to God! Even an entrepreneur, who is completely self-funded, serves and responds to the preferences of his or her customers.

If you are a team member that is often following the lead of others, you can utilize this experience to prepare for the time you get an opportunity to lead a project team or manage a department. If you learn how to become a better follower, and to lead from the middle in certain situations, you will develop important skills for managing and leading in the future.

LeBron James distributes the ball artfully at certain points in the game; he follows the energy and the lead of his teammates. And he steps up to take control at critical moments on the floor or at courtside.

Similarly, the business director sets the agenda and opens the meeting, outlining the desired objectives for the discussion. They are enjoying a strong quarter. He or she walks everyone through the agenda and leads discussion on the first topic: financial results are strong and orders for products are up for the next 90-day period. The product manager on the team leads the next topic. He or she regularly heads up this discussion about quality and delivery metrics while the business director steps back and supports the discussion as needed. He or she is very present in the room, but the conversation is primarily back and forth among other team members. He or she is comfortable following, supporting, encouraging. He or she does not feel the need as the *leader* to be in charge every step of the way.

The authors' review of published books on the topic of leadership resulted in the following breakdown by topic or theme: leadership was mentioned 3,894 times, while followership or follower was mentioned 133 times. The literature is replete with theories, models, and tools to prepare an individual to lead with authority or title from the corner office and from the front. The popular press regularly features segments such as Adam Bryant's Corner Office in *The New York Times* Sunday edition. It is a thoughtful and insightful interview each week with a leader with authority. But there is much less focus in the literature or popular press on following, or followership.

The emergence of the field of followership has been attributed to the scholar Robert Kelley. In his research on followership, Kelley (1988) identified two underlying behavioral dimensions that help identify the difference between followers and nonfollowers. The first behavioral dimension is whether the individual is an independent, critical thinker. The second dimension is whether the individual is active or passive. From these dimensions, Kelley has identified five followership patterns or types of followers:

- Sheep, who have little interest or commitment to the team.

- Yes-People, who conform easily to the direction of the leader.

- Pragmatics, who keep their heads down and do their jobs in the background.

- Alienated, who are naysayers and criticize the leader or team.

- Star Followers, who embrace the team's goals and support the leader, if they respect him or her.

Catalytic team members act as Star Followers who support the leader, mobilize others, and help accelerate progress — taking on task-related leadership responsibilities when appropriate.

WHAT MAKES A GOOD FOLLOWER?

Must you choose in advance for a given situation whether to lead or follow? Not really. Although we have discussed leadership and followership as a dichotomy, where you may not be able to simultaneously engage in both behaviors, that's not necessarily the case. To make the point, consider the interactive process of communicating effectively with another person: we switch between receiving and sending, listening and speaking. If the exchange is positive and effective, we make the switch between those two modes quickly, easily, and seamlessly. Similarly, we can lead from the middle or follow others in a group setting quite effortlessly *if* we have the skill sets necessary for both and *if* we are confident moving nimbly between both roles. (Building good partnerships relies on these skills.)

In our field research for *The Catalyst Effect*, we found that good followers embrace several of the key descriptors that were identified during our in-depth interviews. Valued team members who are viewed as productive followers are most likely to: be results-oriented; care about quality; be willing to step up if needed; encourage others on the team; be good problem solvers; and be someone who will do what it takes to get the job done. The interviewees recognized that not everyone can lead all the time — that following or stepping back to give others room is important to team performance. They value team members who can do this.

As a marketing leader in the arts industry described during our interview, "I think it is similar to the Battier effect because Battier should always be thinking, who's the strongest shooter, who should I be looking for, where should I be? Awareness of people around them and aware of each person's needs and skills becomes crucial to the effective operation of the team. Maybe in our case, I'm the one who needs to take the lead on a project today, but tomorrow a situation will occur that I'm not the most skilled at, so I need to ask for help. In my group, you can do that as a staff-level person. My boss says 'I hired you to do your job, not to do all the jobs.'" (personal communication, 2014)

Factors to Consider When You Decide to Follow and Lead in Real Time

Step Back…

- When others have more knowledge or expertise.

- When you can listen or watch intently to learn more about a situation or skill set.

- When you want to rely on the strength of others.

- When you wish to step back and gain perspective.

- When you want to provide space and support for others to develop skills.

Step Up…

- When you believe your ideas and your experience can add value, share them.

- When you see that the formal leader may want to take a break and "follow" for a while, facilitate.

- When you have the specific tools or skills to improve the team's performance at that moment, offer them.

- When you wish to develop your leadership and facilitation skills, practice them.

Consistent with the idea that good leaders also need to be able to follow, Wharton@Work concludes that "lone leaders" present challenges (Wharton@Work, Executive Education, Leadership, 2012). Their description of a lone leader is the stereotype we have all seen too often where a single individual sets the direction, achieves the results, garners the attention, and accepts all the responsibility. Instead of this stereotype of an incharge, lone leader, they advocate for a leadership ensemble approach. In the ensemble approach, many people will select appropriate times to step into the leadership role and later step back into more of a followership role. That's not unlike the improv example we described at the opening of this chapter.

> *The concept of an ensemble requires that it be filled with people leading from the middle.*
> — Susan Zurbuchan (personal communication, 2015)

Servant Leadership is a theory and approach that embraces several practices similar to the Catalyst Effect. It is based on the work of Robert K. Greenleaf and cites as its underlying philosophy, "The servant-leader *is* servant first.... It begins with the natural feeling that one wants to serve, to serve *first*." (Greenleaf, 1970)

The Greenleaf Center for Servant Leadership focuses on presenting this philosophy and approach to leadership with an emphasis on core skills that include: listening, empathy, healing, awareness, persuasion, conceptualization, foresight, stewardship, commitment to the growth of others, and building community (Servant Leadership Institute, n.d.). Servant Leadership aligns closely with the work of Blake and Mouton (1994) and others who view leadership as highly participatory versus authoritative. Its perspective is still from a leadership position of title or authority versus a role in the middle of the team or organization.

Leadership in other cultures touches on similar values and practices where leadership is viewed as not solely from the front. In the Javanese culture of Indonesia (personal communication, 2016), even though the leader may possess a title and authority, they are encouraged to be able to lead "from the front," "from the back," and "from the middle." The writer most cited as supporting this approach is Ki Hajar Dewantara, a Javanese leadership figure and author. The motto he articulates is used as a foundation for their Education Department today: "(for those) in front should set an example, (for those) in the middle should raise the spirit, and (for those) behind should give encouragement."

As the business environment demands rapid adaptation to changing market conditions and consumer preferences, Spotify takes a unique approach to agile teams which require members to lead or follow at the right times

(Mankins & Garton, 2017). Balancing the concept of control and alignment is central to Spotify's team structure. Spotify is a 12-year-old music, video, and podcast streaming company with 30 million paying subscribers and about $3 billion in revenue. Its over 2,000 employees are organized into agile teams, called *squads*, which are self-organizing and cross-functional. This structure breaks down the typical hierarchical model into agile teams. The teams enable innovation, while keeping the benefits of repeatability. How? Autonomous squads of no more than eight people form to address specific challenges or opportunities. The squads are loosely organized into *tribes* that help connect and support the squads' work and also facilitate learning. Leadership within the squad is self-determined, while the leader is a formal manager who focuses on coaching and mentoring. Spotify believes in the player–coach model: team leaders are also squad members. Because of this structure and the underlying work rules of the squads and tribes, leadership is self-determined by the squad — and the leader must be able to lead or follow quite seamlessly as their roles change from situation to situation, or from group to group (Mankins & Garton, 2017).

Leading and Following in the Operating Room

Let's imagine that you are part of a team that performs surgeries to install pacemakers in heart patients. Typically, the leader in the room with the most authority is the surgeon. But, that doesn't mean that the surgeon should be the one that leads during the entire surgery. Consider two other people in the room that need to know when to lead this team. One such person is the anesthetist. This skilled physician bears primary responsibility for safely sedating the patient. Once the patient is safely sedated, the anesthetist plays a supportive role. But, if there are complications with sedation, the anesthetist will assert himself or herself to have greater influence over the progress of the surgery in order to keep the patient stable.

Another member of the surgery team that will need to assert leadership in a successful pacemaker surgery often isn't an employee of the hospital. Rather, they are technical experts that work for the manufacturer of the pacemaker. These individuals are technical experts on the operation of the device and will sit in on the surgery to help with the installation of the device. For much of the surgery, they will perform a followership role.

> But, at key points in the implant surgery, this individual may need to assert a leadership role to make sure that the device is correctly inserted and is operating properly.

Relinquishing control of a meeting or turning over the responsibility for an aspect of your work to another person can provide needed perspective. Most boards or management teams invite facilitators into their teams to lead the strategic planning process, for instance. This allows the CEO to become a member of the team and to follow the lead of the consultant. Not having to worry about *what we are doing next* can be a valuable way in which team members, including leaders with authority, can step back and gain critical perspective and also make important contributions from a different chair.

We will leave the in-depth discussion of team facilitation skills for another time, but suffice it to say that the tools required to plan and conduct an effective meeting, an effective basketball practice or locker room review, or a rehearsal of new material on stage, are crucial to team performance. They can determine who leads and follows at any given moment. The models and tools for leading effective meetings are well established. The 12 catalytic competencies underlie the ability to use these meeting facilitation tools effectively.

CONCLUSION

We heard Beth describe earlier in this chapter how improv has helped her become more confident and effective — it made her a better catalytic team member and leader.

"By going with an idea that someone else brings to the table, improv puts me in an uncomfortable space where I don't know what's going to happen next. So I can grow and learn from it. We have the mutual respect and trust in one another that enables us to take risks — to know that we will not be criticized, but rather supported! We switch back and forth between leading and following at the right times." (personal communication, 2016)

Catalytic leaders, like good improv players, make "pitches" to other players in ways that drive performance. They have the ability to describe a scene, a vision, and an idea that others can buy into. The passion they bring to the idea inspires others to perform at their very best, leading and following moment by moment.

Take a moment to reflect on your own behavior, do you:

- Use "and" rather than "but" appropriately?

- Move seamlessly between leading from the middle and leading from the front?

- Assess your own comfort level with leading and following? Are you a take-charge person who finds it difficult to sit back and follow others? Are you more laid-back and reluctant to step into a leadership role?

- Examine and develop the skills that are required for you to lead and follow effectively?

- Show your goodwill and leave your baggage at the door?

- Openly discuss with your boss and your team when leadership and followership are each appropriate?

- Invite your boss to understand the value of following, if the situation warrants?

CORNERSTONE 4

AMPLIFYING IMPACT

THE MULTIPLIER EFFECT: SUCCESS REQUIRES COLLECTIVE COMMITMENT

Catalytic behaviors work together to create improved outcomes. They synergistically amplify the impact that individuals and teams have on results. Whether in business, sports, or the arts, exceptional teams have an impact-first approach. The impact may include financial results, points scored and wins tallied, or spectacular performances on stage.

The work associated with amplifying impact is embedded in the team and organizational stories that become the fabric of an organization's culture. How do we drive an uncompromising approach to excellence? Who successfully mentors and coaches our up-and-coming talent? What imaginative ideas emerge to drive innovation and ensure sustainable organizational success?

If you are going to achieve excellence in big things, you develop the habit in little matters. Excellence is not an exception, it is a prevailing attitude.

— Colin Powell in The Leadership Secrets of
Colin Powell (2002)

We have addressed three cornerstones thus far: Building Credibility, Creating Cohesion, and Generating Momentum. Each includes three competencies that were described behaviorally and can be developed with focus and effort. Are these now well established in your tool set? If so, you are in a stronger position to amplify the impact that you have on the team — whether or not you are in a position of formal authority.

Mastery of the competencies in this fourth cornerstone, listed below, will strengthen your ability to lead with steadiness and with urgency when necessary — especially when coupled with a commitment to driving performance.

- Pursues Excellence.

- Mentors and Coaches Others to Excel.

- Proposes Imaginative Solutions.

10

PURSUES EXCELLENCE

Definition: Demonstrates extensive knowledge or competence. Advocates for the high-caliber performance of others.

Counter Behavior: Accepts mediocrity. Seeks to gain advantages over others and to gain undeserved credit.

ACHIEVING EXCELLENCE

Basketball legends are built on the hardwood during March Madness. In this college tourney, excellence on and off the court is celebrated.

The authors explored the following two questions: *How do you make something that is already excellent even better? How do you strive for excellence each and every time you and your team perform?*

Up until the 2009 Men's Final Four, the National Championship Game, had been played in conventional venues — in basketball arenas or with the court placed in one end zone of domed stadiums. This layout allowed for a maximum seating of between 30,000 and 40,000 spectators. According to Tom Jernstedt (personal communication, 2017), who headed the basketball phenomenon for 38 years, tickets were always in short supply. It was difficult to accommodate the enormous fan demand for seats, especially at the semifinals and finals games. To increase the impact of the tournament nationally, a decision was made to move to an unconventional seating configuration to meet the tremendous demand for tickets.

For the 2009 tournament, the Division I Men's Basketball Championship Committee made the leap of faith to grow the tournament by conducting the Final Four games in a full dome set, with the court placed at the center of the field. This configuration included an additional 20,000 seats brought closer to the floor, opening up other permanent seats that were closed in the half-dome configuration. This allowed attendance to double. It was important that this new approach work, particularly for the host city, Detroit, which was going through some hard times and needed to stimulate its economy. Even more, the people of the state of Michigan and city of Detroit wanted to have an event of this stature to celebrate the community, college basketball, and excellence.

In 1979, the Michigan State versus Indiana State NCAA Division I Men's Basketball National Championship Game in Salt Lake City featured Larry Bird and Magic Johnson. It was an important and memorable time for the sport. At the time, many considered Bird one of the best collegiate players ever, while Magic orchestrated the Michigan State team brilliantly as a 6′ 9″ point guard — with leadership and charisma to boot. (Michigan State fans reading this story will of course recall that they won that game.)

It is now April 2009 in Detroit. Magic and Larry are both invited back to attend the championship game for a ceremonial pregame ball presentation. It is an amazing crowd of 72,922 at Ford Field and a memorable experience for fans, student-athletes, staff, and locals, as North Carolina beat Michigan State in the championship game.

Working to support something so large was very personal for many in Detroit and for the NCAA staff as well: Could they successfully pull off this enormous event? Pride was present in everything that was done. Given the magnitude of the challenge, the NCAA staff and Detroit Local Organizing Committee brought their very best team performance to make all of this happen seamlessly. The 2009 Final Four proved to be the road map for future men's basketball championship events that are still in place today.

Two members of the NCAA staff at that time, Lee Dicklitch and Tom Jernstedt, explained to the authors in 2017 the impact of that year's championship from different perspectives. Dicklitch served as an associate director on the staff working on his first championship, while Jernstedt had overseen an incredible period of growth as the executive vice president of Championships that few events in the world could rival in magnitude. They both described the full commitment their team had to making the event nothing short of superb as they took the risk to expand attendance. Substantial financial benefits to the community accrued, while sponsorships, ticket revenue, and most importantly, the student-athlete and fan experiences each reached new levels of excellence.

To this day, March Madness continues to represent a passion for college athletics that is unlike any annual tradition in the world. It involves literally thousands of athletes, university staff, NCAA staff, corporate sponsors, and partners at 13 cities across the country. There is no doubt the Final Four has been a shining star among major sporting events for decades: basketball legends are established, underdogs often prevail, games are won or lost on dramatic final shots, university fans gather to support their teams, and catalysts are identified!

Assuming responsibility for organizing and operating one of the world's major sporting events is no small challenge.

For the NCAA Men's Final Four, the challenge was, and is, to take the event to the next level of excellence each and every year and to inspire all involved to perform at their best — this is the essence of the Catalyst Effect.

Two key themes consistently underpin the tournament:

1. The event is first and foremost about the student-athletes and the students of the participating institutions.

2. The tournament is always excellent, and it can always be improved!

It is the drive to inspire excellence by everyone involved in the tournament that we will explore in this chapter.

HOW THE 2014 NCAA TEAM INSPIRED PERFORMANCE

In conversations with Jernstedt and Dicklitch, the authors learned that the NCAA staff working on the championship each year was a very talented and competitive group committed to administering the tournament at the highest level possible. Leading them was not unlike coaching a team of high-performing athletes, so the challenge was to tap the enormous energy and competitiveness of the staff while getting them to work together to improve the performance of their team. This was where the glue-guys and glue-gals on the team came in. They balanced the incredible drive of the individuals with the drumbeat of *this is about the student-athletes, and it's about our team working together to serve them.*

As the leader of the group, Jernstedt built on this drive. As an individual who appreciated the importance of getting the details right, he set an example for thoroughness and excellence in everything the staff did.

> *MARCH MADNESS! THE FINAL FOUR! How did it happen?*
> *When did it start? Tom Jernstedt is the answer to how and when.*
> *Over nearly four decades Tom through his catalytic leadership*
> *style was the architect of what has made men's college basketball*
> *the owner of the biggest event in sports. Thank God that Tom*
> *and our great game were intimate friends!*
>
> — Mike Krzyzewski

Jernstedt set a high bar for almost four decades. There is a reverence and respect for the tradition of March Madness built on his legacy, as well as the commitment and excellence of the players and coaches who dedicate so much. The clear goal of the NCAA staff has been to improve the tournament each year. Team goals are clear, individual job responsibilities are reviewed and adjusted to fit the needs of the moment, each member expects the best of every person on the team, and they trust and expect each other to deliver at a high level.

It's a well-worn maxim that most people don't like attending meetings; they often see them as a waste of time and motion. Meetings are often the norm and expected in large organizations such as the NCAA. As Lee Dicklitch commented, "[T]he team understood that our meetings often could go very deep into the details to ensure everything was coming together successfully. We knew that each responsibility had to be done at the highest level to ensure the tournament would continue to improve. The internal dialogue in team meetings was often very candid and intricate. Tom and the other leaders on our team pushed us to focus narrowly on the details, execute the expectations of the championship broadly, and trusted us to elevate the event to even higher standards in the future." (personal communication, 2017)

To be excellent, there must be very little wasted motion. Everyone was there for everyone else whenever they needed help. The entire team, from the executive vice president to the intern, *expected the best of each other, nothing less*!

They committed *to pursuing excellence!*

EXCELLENCE: WHAT DOES IT LOOK LIKE?

You likely know someone who simply refuses to accept anything less than an excellent performance or outcome. We saw in the NCAA example that team members would simply not accept anything other than outstanding performance from themselves and their peers. This extraordinary commitment to excellence was also a catalytic characteristic mentioned by many of our field research participants. Whether their role was performing on stage, playing in the arena, or solving problems in the conference room, the interviewees stressed that demonstration of personal excellence was essential.

At the organizational level of performance, Tom Peters and Robert Waterman in their well-known book, *In Search of Excellence* (1982), identified firms that they defined as pursuing and delivering excellence. They noted eight attributes that such firms have in common.

1. A bias for action, active decision-making: Facilitate quick decision-making and problem-solving; tends to avoid bureaucratic control.

2. Close to the customer: Learning from the people served by the business.

3. Autonomy and entrepreneurship: Fostering innovation and nurturing champions.

4. Productivity through people: Treating rank-and-file employees as a source of quality.

5. Hands-on and value-driven management philosophy that guides everyday practice; management showing its commitment.

6. Stick to the knitting: Stay with the business that you know.

7. Simple form, lean staff: Some of the best companies have minimal headquarter staff.

8. Simultaneous loose—tight properties: Autonomy in shop floor activities plus centralized values.

A study conducted 20 years later shows the performance difference between firms on Peters' and Waterman's *Excellence* list as compared to the Dow Jones Industrial Average (DJIA). By 2002, a $10,000 investment made in 1982 in the 34 firms on the *Excellence* list would have yielded $140,050.

A similar investment in the DJIA would have only yielded $85,500 (Ackman, 2002).

The importance of the Peters and Waterman work was its focus on how companies actually achieve excellence. It sparked a surge in the analysis of best practices across companies that continue to this day. There remains an intense curiosity as to how sports teams or business teams outperform others. What is the magic sauce?

UNDERSTANDING AND MEASURING ORGANIZATIONAL EXCELLENCE

Catalysts focus on team excellence and understand why and how *organizations and teams* achieve it. By understanding the criteria for organizational excellence, catalysts apply their personal skills to influence the drive for it.

A proven approach to assessing excellence in organizations has been the Malcolm Baldrige Criteria and Award. An article titled "Baldrige Framework and Value System," posted by Partners in Performance Excellence, notes that "[t]he Baldrige Criteria provide a systems perspective for managing the organization and its key processes to achieve the right results while striving for performance excellence." (Partners in Performance Excellence, Catalyst for Success, n.d.) It provides a framework for managing the whole organization, as well as its components, to achieve success. This is an important value that Baldrige has uniquely created and freely offers to leaders with the wisdom to see it. The Baldrige Criteria have three important roles that strengthen an organization's ability to be innovative, competitive, and sustainable:

1. Help improve organizational performance practices, capabilities, and results.

2. Facilitate communication and sharing of information on best practices among organizations of all types.

3. Serve as a working tool for understanding and managing performance and for guiding organizational planning and opportunities for learning.

The Baldrige Criteria are relevant for all organizations, not just manufacturing where it was applied originally. The values and concepts are embedded beliefs and behaviors found in excellent, high-performing organizations across all disciplines. So, whether you are focusing on business, not for profits, the arts, or sports, these criteria integrate key performance requirements within a framework that drives for results. These criteria include specific metrics and provide a basis for action and feedback. They are as follows:

- Visionary leadership.

- Customer-driven excellence.

- Organizational and personal learning.

- Valuing workforce members and partners.

- Agility.

- Focus on the future.

- Managing for innovation.

- Management by fact.

- Societal responsibility.

- Focus on results and creating value.

- Systems perspective.

We encourage you to explore the Baldrige framework and consider how you can apply the measureable standards to your organization (Partners in Performance Excellence, Catalyst for Success, n.d.).

As you consider the organizational aspects of excellence along with the individual characteristics, remember that fast-paced and top-performing organizations require best practice organizational processes. These can be applied to symphony rehearsals and performances, customer service, education, or product delivery.

THE INDIVIDUAL DRIVE FOR EXCELLENCE

To better understand why some people are driven to excellence, it is important to understand what drives them. Two qualities are critical: focus and passion.

Focus

Focus, being fully present in the here and now, is key to performing well. According to Dr. Kristen Race, "Mindfulness helps train the prefrontal cortex, the part of the brain that creates a calm and alert state of mind, which helps us stay focused, avoid distraction and perform at our best." (cited in Yu, 2014) She says, "It's one of the best ways to calm the stress response in the brain. This allows us to notice our thoughts and emotions without getting attached to them." (cited in Yu, 2014)

Focus drives excellence because it brings to bear all the capabilities someone possesses and concentrates them on a single skill, task, or objective. And, it does so in a sustained way. In Goleman's recent book on focus, he notes that attention to task is an underappreciated skill that helps create excellent outcomes (Goleman, 2013). He also notes that it is a disappearing skill set. He observes that many of us allow social media and mobile devices to distract and interrupt our thinking.

Are we training our children to be less focused as Goleman (2013) contends?

At a recent children's dance recital attended by one of the authors, a boy of about six was sitting on his mother's lap holding a tablet device and a set of over-ear headphones. On the screen, he was watching a cartoon. Perhaps there were extenuating circumstances of which we were unaware, but the point is, despite the recital being presented in two segments of 45 minutes each, separated by a 10-minute intermission, the boy was *assumed* to be unable to be engaged or focused. This was a performance by other children, many of whom he likely knew, dancing their hearts out in all manner of sparkle and color. Next to the kid watching the video were two adults playing a Connect-Four game on their phones.

Are our attention spans really so short? And just to check: How many times have you stopped reading this book or this chapter to see if you have a new e-mail or text?

Passion and Commitment

Passionate people dedicate themselves to their craft. Many people assume that the exploits of highly successful musicians are almost exclusively the result of remarkable natural talent. However, scientists conducting expert performance research (Ericsson, 2006) suggest that individuals such as those mentioned in this book have achieved high levels of performance because they have engaged for several years in highly structured practice aimed at improvement and skill refinement. Indeed, it is often forgotten that these individuals had to work hard at their craft, often for years before finally making it.

Excellence is the by-product of people who take the time to really work on getting better and do so in a systematic way. In studies utilizing music students, Ericsson and a team of investigators spent considerable effort looking at how students attained mastery of their instruments (Ericsson, 2006; Ericsson, Krampe, & Tesch-Römer, 1993). They examined all aspects of musical instrument performance mastery and concluded that deliberate practice was the most important of all the reasons a musician would achieve excellence. Adding further to the analysis, they concluded that, assuming all the requisite physical skills were there, it would take someone a minimum of 10,000 hours to become an expert (Ericsson, Prietula, & Cokely, 2007). Virtually all of the symphony musicians that we interviewed began playing their instruments at an early age. Their primary focus and passion in life was to perform at an extraordinary level from grade school through their current position in the orchestra.

Said another way, you can't just play golf for 10,000 hours or write computer code and expect mastery. The hours need to be dedicated to deliberate, focused skill development. A recent example of intense practice aimed at mastery was described in *The New York Times*. Most of us have heard the phrase *standing on one foot*. It is a colloquial phrase intended to suggest an added level of difficulty to any activity. However, in this case, it wasn't just a colloquialism. In a practice that took place prior to Game 2 of the 2017 NBA finals, a writer described Kevin Durant practicing:

> *The latest superstar addition to the Golden State Warriors balanced on one foot about 18 feet from the basket. An assistant tossed the basketball at him, which he caught without losing his balance. Then, still on one foot, he shot at the basket. Durant hit about 80 percent of those shots.*
>
> — Powell (2017)

If you are not an NBA player, you would likely struggle to hit 80% of your shots from 10 feet even if you use the traditional two-handed, two-footed jump shot. As an indication of his pursuit of excellence, Kevin Durant managed to do that standing on one foot, 18 feet from the basket.

Incidentally, in a dominant performance over the Cleveland Cavaliers later that night, Durant hit at least two shots, falling to the ground, off one foot. In one, he had an opposing player draped around his waist. The announcers were incredulous at the unlikelihood of hitting such shots. They probably didn't realize that Durant's performance wasn't simply a function of thousands of hours of traditional shots, he had also engaged in a dedicated practice activity to acquire and master the skill of shooting off one foot. Although, it is hard to imagine that he practiced it with an opponent draped around his waist!

For a musician, achieving excellence may be about being in the moment. Several interviewees from the Indianapolis Symphony Orchestra confirmed to us that they experience *edge of the seat* moments on stage. They describe them as a bit otherworldly. Somewhat levitating. The orchestra is perfectly connected as one. "The conductor leads us right up to the edge of being out of control, yet we are still bonded together. And the bonus is when we know that the audience is experiencing the music with us in a similar way; that they are on the edges of their seats as well."

Passion and Grit

How gritty are you? Angela Duckworth's (2016) research has been focused on exceptional performance and success. Specifically, she studies why some individuals accomplish much more than others even though their skills and talent are similar. She highlights the importance of having passion for long-term goals and the tenacity to aggressively pursue them.

She also draws a contrast between excellence and perfection. She postulates that gritty people don't necessarily seek perfection, but rather strive for excellence (Duckworth, 2016). It may seem that these two have only subtle semantic distinctions, yet they are quite different.

Perfection can be viewed as excellence's somewhat burdensome first cousin. It is unforgiving and inflexible. The drive for perfection can then become a barrier to excellence rather than an enabling factor. Excellence, on the other hand, is a desire and commitment to achieving the highest level of mastery possible. It is not an endgame per se but is demonstrated in how one fulfills a purpose. It is forgiving and can even embrace failure and vulnerability as part of the ongoing quest for improvement. The pursuit of excellence allows for mistakes and for learning from our failures; it prioritizes *progress over perfection.*

> *I simply strived to play so well and with such intensity, to play so hard, that coach could not afford to take me off the floor.*
> — Shane Battier (personal communication, 2015)

Duckworth also notes that a highly self-controlled person who may never step out of line (who may be too worried about making an error) may fail to reach the same heights as their passionate but more flexible colleagues because they simply will not push themselves to take a risk in order to improve. She suggests that it is more important to go for the gold than just show up for rehearsal or practice (Duckworth, 2016).

An additional distinction between someone who succeeds and someone who is just spending a lot of time doing something is this: practice must have purpose. That's where long-term goals come in. They provide the framework in which you find the raison dêtre of your long-term efforts, which help sustain your commitment to getting better every day...to excellence.

Don't be afraid to do the hard thing!

CONCLUSION

Perhaps if we practiced deliberately as much as we watched TV or spent time on Facebook, mastery could more easily be in reach. The idea that most people simply do not have time to master skills is questionable. What's missing is motivation and discipline, along with an understanding of how the skills you seek are mastered. Ask yourself, after you have spent significant time on social media and watching entertaining shows, what have you gained? Are you closer to your goals? If you had devoted some of that time to pursuing excellence, how much farther along might you be? Maintaining your focus, as well as the focus of your team, takes extraordinary discipline if you want to achieve excellence. You can provide this as a catalytic leader by finding ways to keep the team focused and motivated.

Don't be afraid to do the hard thing! Practice is often hard: it requires sustained focus, passion, and energy. Mastery requires thoughtful practice (perhaps up to 10,000 hours!). Changes are usually incremental. Practice can test the limits of our muscles and brains, and for most people, a four-hour practice session feels like a marathon.

Consider Duckworth's (2016) "Hard Thing Rule" for yourself. In short, there are three parts: "First, everyone on the team or in the family must participate in selecting something new to learn. Second, you can quit if you don't like it, or you think it is too hard, but you can't quit until the season is over! You must finish what you have started; you can't just quit because you have a bad day. And third, only *you* can select your hard thing. It defeats the purpose if someone else picks it for you." (Duckworth, 2016, pp. 241–242)

Identify a hard thing. Try it. Get better. Happy learning.

Take a moment to reflect on your own behavior, do you:

- Commit to being a person who pursues excellence and is hungry to learn?

- Identify what excellence looks like for you in your field or your current job? Who are current examples of excellence and what are their profiles?

- Dedicate large chunks of time throughout your day on focused, uninterrupted work?

- Identify two skills you currently have that you want to improve? Set measurable improvement goals for these skills.

- Identify two skills that you don't have that you want to learn? Commit to learning these new skills one at a time over the next several months.

- Find someone that can help you with deliberate practice techniques, i.e., someone who will help keep you accountable for becoming excellent?

11

MENTORS AND COACHES OTHERS TO EXCEL

Definition: Models exemplary behavior and supports the personal and professional development of others by providing constructive advice.

Counter Behaviors: Focused on self; does not share knowledge or techniques with others; does not pass on what others have taught.

A NURSE WHO IS EAGER TO ADVANCE

Jenny: A young psychiatric nurse.

Ruth: The manager of Jenny's department.

Sal: Jenny's mentor at the hospital.

Evan: Jenny's professional leadership coach.

The roles of supervisors, mentors, and coaches are different. Each can be key to the development of catalytic skills for emerging leaders. The three roles overlap to some extent, but in Jenny's case the opportunity to build relationships with three different individuals who played different roles in her career was invaluable. Ruth was a capable *supervisor*, but did not have the passion nor the patience to be the indispensable mentor that Sal was. Sal was a superb *mentor*, but did not have the skill set or the objectivity to help Jenny develop her skills in a very specific, well-planned manner. The introduction of Evan, a professional *leadership coach* was vital to Jenny's development and career success.

Jenny recalls her early experience in nursing as she aspired to advance into a supervisory role:

> I was 27 and had just graduated as a Registered Nurse a few months earlier. I already had my LPN and 3-4 years of work experience so I felt that I was ready to apply for an assistant manager's role in the psychiatric unit where I worked. I anxiously awaited the decision of the selection team. The bottom line was that I did not get the job. They promoted a peer of mine into the role, which triggered several hours — even days — of soul searching on my part as to what I was lacking in my skill set. The individual they selected had no more experience than I did, but obviously the selection team saw something in her that I was missing. What was it?
>
> Fortunately, Ruth, my department manager, invited me into her office to talk about my disappointment. She correctly assumed that I was feeling down and a bit confused. Ruth was candid with me. She outlined the requirements for the role and the strengths that the other candidate brought to it. Somewhat to my surprise and appreciation, she also was prepared to highlight the gaps in my skills and competencies. She constructively and specifically discussed three areas of feedback. First was the need for the assistant manager to handle difficult and sometimes contentious discussions with junior staff in the unit, some of whom were many years older than me. The selection team saw me as a bit too hesitant and laid-back to be able to address these situations proactively. Second, the role also required scheduling and planning skills via the unit's software system. I had decent technical skills but had not taken the initiative to participate in the relevant training workshops that had been offered earlier in the year. Third, the selection team viewed the other candidate as having more "leadership presence." That comment confused me, and hurt a bit — it felt like a personal criticism. When I asked Ruth what she meant by that, she quickly indicated that she had not meant to offend me (she noticed my reaction) and that she would try to explain or describe the behaviors that led her to that conclusion. It was on that attempt to be more specific that she got off track and was unable to provide me with constructive, useful input. Ruth essentially said it boiled down to the other person

acting more like a leader at this point in time. Being the competitive
person I am, I was committed to understanding what it took to
advance, what my gaps were, and then taking the steps necessary to
improve. (personal communication, 2017)

MANAGING AND SUPERVISING

Ruth provided Jenny with valuable feedback and insight into why she did
not get the job. She served as a capable manager and supervisor at that point
in Jenny's career. Ruth was less capable of providing input to Jenny on the
somewhat vague idea of *leadership presence.* She was repeating what the
selection team had mentioned. In truth, neither the selection team nor Ruth
had clearly identified the underlying behaviors that were associated with the
leadership skills needed for the assistant manager's position. Nor had they
identified the specific catalytic competencies and behaviors that served as the
foundation for effective leaders at the hospital.

MENTORING

Ruth also did something for Jenny at the end of that initial difficult conversation that may have changed the course of Jenny's career. Ruth suggested that
Jenny could benefit from having a mentor. Someone who could provide
input about the organization and provide some hints about how to navigate
the career ladder at the hospital — someone who understood how to help
Jenny develop *leadership* or *executive presence* in the context of the hospital
system. A mentor who could be a sounding board for Jenny when or if she
was frustrated and could be a cheerleader for her when she experienced success. Sal was that mentor. She had *seen everything* over the years and at age
48 had made the decision to step out of middle-level management roles and
go back into direct patient service and support. Sal served as a confidant; a
navigator of the organization's dynamics and politics. She was an advisor to
Jenny — suggesting who to approach and when with her suggestions for
improvements in work processes. She also let Jenny know who was a strong
proponent of quality performance and continuous improvement approaches
and tools.

Sal had stepped down from a middle-level manager's role a couple of years earlier because she found the pressure of dealing with supervisory issues a bit too stressful. In addition, she was now a grandmother and was devoting time to helping her daughter with evening and weekend childcare. Her dedication to helping others grow was well recognized and valued by the organization. At her retirement party at age 55, she was presented with the Mentor of the Decade award in recognition of all the people she had supported over the years. Sal was a superb model of catalytic competencies, particularly her ability to connect emotionally, be selfless, elevate the performance of others, and energize her mentees. As a result, others gained not only from what she said but also from watching how she behaved.

COACHING

Ruth's additional suggestion to Jenny was to work with a professional leadership coach. This coach, Evan, had played a key role in Ruth's development and she thought that Jenny could benefit as well.

She gave Evan's contact information to Jenny and encouraged her to meet with him to identify and address her skill gaps. It was also an opportunity for her to sort out career questions regarding her level of commitment to being a manager versus a long-term professional psychiatric nurse. Evan worked outside of the organization but knew the dynamics of the hospital and the key leaders quite well. With his support, Jenny completed two assessments to understand herself and her interpersonal style more fully: one was a personality instrument and the other was a conflict management indicator. The coach also interviewed Ruth and Sal to gain their insights as to what skills Jenny could benefit from improving. This objective, external input was extremely valuable as Evan asked questions that assessed many of what we have identified as catalytic competencies and behaviors.

With that input in hand, Jenny and Evan laid out a specific development plan that she implemented over the next 12 months. It included technical training on the software system, a series of workshops on communication skills and conflict management, and a series of 10, full-day seminars focused on women's career achievement and the development of leadership skills.

JENNY: REFLECTIONS ON HER SITUATION

As Ruth advanced into more senior roles at the hospital over the next several years, she was able to support Jenny for additional developmental assignments and larger jobs. She brought Jenny to the attention of the hospital's senior executive team as a high potential individual who could grow successfully into more challenging leadership roles.

Jenny possessed the basic catalytic skills related to teamwork and a strong desire to learn more: she was extremely coachable. Her excellent communication skills, optimism, ability to connect emotionally with peers, selflessness, and commitment to excellence served as a strong foundation for success. With Sal helping her to navigate the organization, Evan working with Jenny more deeply on conflict management and organizational skills, and Ruth continuing to support her career growth, Jenny thrived over the next decade.

Fast forward, she ultimately became a vice president at the hospital.

If you reflect on your personal and professional development, you likely have one or more people in mind that influenced you positively and deeply. Perhaps they took a keen interest in you when others did not; maybe they pointed out that you have talent(s) that you should strive to develop; perhaps they provided assurance and comfort during a tough time; or they might have shared advice, a key learning, that changed how you think about things.

As you read this chapter, we invite you to reflect on those situations in which a mentor or coach made a difference in your life. As you revisit those moments, try to remember the specifics of the situation. How did they engage you? What were their words to you? How did their influence spur your progress?

The skills of coaching and mentoring integrate many of the competencies we have discussed earlier — in order to mentor or coach others effectively, you need to have mastered many or most of them.

THE SKILLS OF OUTSTANDING MENTORS AND COACHES

Although not all catalytic competencies are dependent on the presence of others, this one is. What we mean is that this competency will rely on your ability to be skilled at other competencies in order for it to have maximum

effect. Two competencies that we discussed in earlier chapters also character-
ize effective mentoring relationships: the abilities to connect emotionally and
to engender trust (Chun, Litzky, Sosik, Bechtold, & Godshalk, 2010).

Mentoring and coaching are only effective to the extent that the mentor
or coach can successfully connect with the employee or team member
through an accurate understanding of their mind-set, as well as their feelings
or apprehensions. The first, crucial task for the mentor or coach is to understand the other person's frame of reference, their perspectives, and while
doing so, establish an open, trusting relationship.

Coaching is frequently done by the boss or by peers who have specific skills
in their catalyst tool kits. Even though the nature of the relationship between
coach and coachee is different when it is the boss or a peer versus a professional coach, the foundational skills that underlie both professional coaching
and less formal organizational coaching or mentoring are largely the same.
The major differences lie in the objectivity of the professional coach, thoroughness of assessment, formality of meeting arrangements, and the fee.

Successful mentoring and coaching relationships have a lot in common: both
are established through initial nonthreatening, supportive discussions. The
how-to of both mentoring and coaching relationships involves mastering the art
of asking great questions, clarifying assumptions, being fully present, carefully
listening to both the content and feelings in the discussions, probing and challenging constructively, and sensitively sharing your perspectives. As mentioned
previously, the mastery of several of the earlier catalytic competencies is crucial.

How do you get the most from a relationship with a good coach or
mentor? It requires that you come to the relationship with an open and
curious mind — with a focus on communicating clearly and connecting
effectively with your mentor or coach.

A supervisor in a visual arts organization commented to us in her interview, "I welcome coaching from the folks in my group. From staff to boss
and vice versa. I have a very vocal staff. They have done a great job of
coaching me when they think they can help. Some leaders are not willing to
accept that kind of coaching. I call it *upward coaching*." (personal communication, 2015) This individual values her staff's input. She recognizes that
others have strengths and experience that may be more relevant than her
own, to her great benefit and her development as a supervisor.

Bosses need sounding boards as well. Can you develop such a valued role
for your boss, your coach, or your team leader? Are you comfortable doing

so if asked or if you see an opportunity to add value? How might you broach the subject? How do you become a great mentor or coach to others, whether a peer or supervisor?

> *In order to be a mentor, and an effective one, one must care. You must care. You don't have to know how many square miles are in Idaho, you don't need to know what is the chemical makeup of chemistry, or of blood or water. Know what you know and care about the person, care about what you know and care about the person you're sharing with.*
>
> — Maya Angelou, interview,
> https://sites.sph.harvard.edu/wmy/celebrities/maya-angelou/

MENTORING AND COACHING IN PRACTICE

To illustrate the power of strong coaching/mentoring initiatives in organizations, let's consider the not-for-profit organization InHerSight. The organization's mission is to address the working conditions of and opportunities for women in organizations across the country.

One key metric that they track is whether a mentoring program has been established in the organization. The data they have collected on mentoring show a clear link between excellent mentoring and job satisfaction. They also note that, by extension, a good mentoring program can reduce turnover. Firms that have received high marks for their programs include NetSuite and PayPal. Employees are enthusiastic about them, and the firms are planning to expand the programs (InHerSight, Fast Company).

Although there are many qualities, caveats, and conditions described in the studies of coaching and mentoring, these activities are without question seen as broadly effective ways of improving the skill sets of individuals. Much of this work has been focused on informal relationships. As this work has been documented, organizations have moved quickly to create formal programs as a way of extending and accelerating the effect of developmental relationships (Weinberg & Lankau, 2011).

> *It is not, nor ever, about you; it is about the individual you are supporting.*
>
> — Bacon and Voss (Adaptive Coaching, 2012)

For our purposes, we are less concerned with these and more concerned with informal systems. We hold this orientation for two reasons. First, it is our strongly held belief that as catalytic leaders, you can lead from anywhere. In a formalized program, you may not be considered for a coaching or mentoring role as a function of youth, limited years of experience, or the fact that the number of people you supervise is small or nonexistent. When organizations participate in formalized programs, they often fall victim to old stereotypes and only select coaches from the pool of people that have historically been thought of as leaders. They have years of experience and lofty titles. You may not fit that description and therefore may not be asked to participate in the firm's coaching program. If you are considered, it is more likely that you will be considered for the coachee role. Let us be clear, if your organization offers you the chance to be mentored by a C-suite officer, TAKE IT! Taking it doesn't mean that you need to limit your thinking about your value as a coach or mentor to others.

The other reason we persist in encouraging you to explore coaching and mentoring roles outside a formal system is that, according to some scholars, informal coaching and mentoring systems are more effective than formal systems (Chao, Walz, & Gardner, 1992). Likely because informal activities grow more organically, the fit between coach and protégé is better, and the two people more committed to the outcomes. Also, populating a mentoring program with the most senior titles in the organization neglects to recognize that these individuals already have tremendous demands on their time. It is possible that the protégé becomes just another relationship that the senior executive needs to manage.

With respect to catalytic opportunities to coach and mentor, the use of senior people is no longer seen as the only method. A recent *Harvard Business Review* book titled *Coaching and Mentoring: How to Develop Top Talent and Achieve Higher Performance* describes how peer mentoring works and notes its effectiveness either as a stand-alone activity or as one combined with other potentially senior mentors (*Harvard Business Review*, 2004). This multiple mentor approach is referred to as *network mentoring* and it currently is very much in vogue. It recognizes that few mentors may possess the full array of skills and experiences necessary.

MENTORING AND COACHING IN ORGANIZATIONAL SETTINGS: WHAT ARE THE DIFFERENCES?

You might think mentoring and coaching are similar or even the same thing. They are not. According to Management Mentors (n.d.) there are several key differentiators:

1. **Coaching is more task-oriented.** The focus is usually on specific issues, such as managing conflict more effectively, speaking in a more polished manner in front of groups, or learning how to develop a strategic plan. This requires a content expert (a coach) who is capable of helping an individual develop these skills.

   Mentoring is more relationship-oriented. It seeks to provide a safe environment where the mentee shares issues that affect his or her professional and personal success in the organization. Although specific learning goals or competencies may be used as a basis for creating the relationship, its focus goes beyond these areas to include other matters, such as work/life balance, self-confidence, self-perception, and how the personal influences the professional.

2. **Coaching is short(er) term.** A coach can successfully be involved with an individual for a short period of time, maybe even just a few discussions. The coaching simply lasts for as long as is needed, depending on the goals of the coaching relationship.

   Mentoring is long(er) term. Mentoring usually requires time during which both partners can learn about one another and build a climate of trust. The employee must feel secure in sharing the real issues that impact his or her success. Successful mentoring relationships last months or years.

3. **Coaching is usually performance-driven.** The purpose of coaching is to improve the individual's performance on the job. This involves either enhancing current skills or acquiring new skills.

   Mentoring is more development-driven. Its purpose is to develop the individual not only for the current job but also for future roles in the organization. Mentors may assist the individual in navigating the progression or jungle gym of job progression in the organization.

4. **In coaching, the immediate manager of the employee is a key partner or sponsor.** He or she often provides the coach with feedback on areas in which the employee will benefit from development. The coach uses this information to guide the coaching process and to assess progress.

In mentoring, the immediate manager is less directly involved. Although he or she may offer suggestions to the employee on how to best use the mentoring experience or may provide a recommendation to the matching committee on what would constitute a good match, the manager usually has no direct link to or feedback from the mentor.

Consider Coaching When

- Employees seek assistance in developing specific competencies needed in new roles.

- An individual needs to prepare for a challenge or a position they have not faced before.

- An employee is not performing as well as expected. Who would benefit from assessing why and determining how to close the gap between current and expected skill utilization?

- A leader needs assistance in acquiring a new skill as an additional, broader responsibility.

- A high potential, emerging leader needs to rapidly develop his or her management skill set.

Consider Mentoring When

- The transfer of certain skills and knowledge from current, mature employees to younger individuals in the organization is desired.

- Specific groups of employees can benefit from navigating the unwritten rules or dynamics in an organization.

- New employees or new team members need to come up to speed quickly and successfully.

- Personal, supportive relationships can foster confidence building and connections.

How Intel Approaches Mentoring

Intel has been a leader in establishing mentoring programs. The company matches people not by job title or years of service, but by the expertise needed by the recipient. It goes beyond the usual (and often valuable) programs that organizations put in place to help foster the career growth of employees, especially high potentials. It focuses on *what* you want to learn, not on *who* you know.

Intel's lead mentor in New Mexico described the program as not a special program for special people as described in an article for Fast Company (Warner, 2002). Nor is the company's mentoring-with-a-difference process all about face time and one-on-one relationships. Instead, Intel uses intranet and e-mail to perform the matchmaking, creating relationships that may stretch across state lines and national boundaries. This enables Intel to spread best practices and build important relationships quickly throughout the far-flung organization. Intel uses written contracts and tight deadlines to make sure that its mentoring program quickly produces results. The program's success hinges on how well knowledge is passed along to a new generation.

Intel's previous mentoring programs had not gained the desired traction and sustainability. This "e-approach" has stuck in part because it fits the faster-paced changes needed in the tech industry and addresses the mentoring needs of the vast majority of employees, rather than primarily high potentials or just those assertive enough to seek out a mentor.

Once a match is made, an automatic e-mail goes to the mentor asking him or her to set up a time to talk. The mentor and the partner also are given basic guidelines vital to the relationship (Warner, 2002).

1. The partner (mentee) controls the relationship. Partners, not mentors, set up meetings and decide what they want to work on. According to Intel, mentoring relationships that last from six to nine months work best.

2. The objectives of the relationship are outlined in a mentoring contract. While not binding, that contract creates accountability that goes far beyond traditional mentoring relationships.

3. Both the partner and the mentor decide what to discuss. Once formality is out of the way, candor and privacy take over. The limits of what can and can't be discussed are set by the partner and the mentor together, not by the people who run the program. This frees them up to bounce ideas around as "what if's," to privately question ideas, to gain a different perspective about a technical issue, relationship concerns, the mentee's next job opportunity, and anything else of importance.

Unlike many corporations that use mentoring for career advancement, Intel's approach is about learning from someone whom the employee has perhaps never met, who may be a peer at another location, or a highly accomplished professional whom they can approach via text or e-mail. And it is open to everyone, from workers on the factory floor to senior-level engineers and managers.

Reinforcing Leaders Who Pay It Forward

Here is an example of a company who recognizes mentors who pay it forward. One of the authors had the opportunity to codevelop a global recognition program for employees who served as exemplary developers of talent. The objective of the program in this 30,000+ employee organization was to emphasize the importance of employee growth in skills and impact by featuring those employees, whether supervisors or peers, who made a significant difference in other employees' development. Only 1 in approximately 5,000 employees would be recognized at a global event. Called the Genesis Award for Excellence in People Development, the criteria were as follows:

- Rewarding the skills of people development at all levels.

- Appreciating diverse people development styles and learning from unique geographical and cultural strengths.

- Ensuring an objective selection process that allowed every employee to be considered for the award.

Nominations were by peers, and the review and selection teams were composed of well-respected mentors and coaches globally.

The Genesis Award Program ran successfully for well over a decade with minor tweaks and adjustments. It more recently has evolved into the Olympus Award for Superior People Leadership, retaining the emphasis on the leadership behaviors that enhance employee success and highlighting those leaders, at all levels, who positively impact others' development.

Coaching Olympic Athletes

A study by the Canadian Olympic Committee (as cited in Hanson, n.d.) on coach–athlete relationships reveals practices that can be applied anywhere, not just in sports. Penny Werthner, herself an Olympic athlete, concludes that to produce Olympic champions, coaches must deliver in five critical areas (as cited in Hanson, n.d.):

Build your employee's development plan on her natural talents and interests. Work with each individual to accurately identify strengths, not on remediation of weaknesses. What really excites and interests them? How does he or she like to be rewarded? How do they like to be challenged? Note: for more information and assessments pertaining to strengths, see StrengthsFinder by Rath (2007).

> *From the cradle to the cubicle, we devote more time to our shortcomings than to our strengths.*
>
> — Tom Rath (2007)

Create a relationship of trust and respect. This is the foundation of successful work collaboration and was cited as "the most crucial factor in winning an Olympic Medal or producing a personal best performance." Demonstrate the willingness to listen to whatever is shared. Create a pattern of honest, two-way communication. Don't be afraid to show weaknesses and be who *you* are. Be willing to share your coaching role with others as needed. Leverage your vantage point as coach by pulling in additional individuals who have expertise you may lack but your employee needs.

Audit your employee's world at work. Are they connected to other key players who can help him or her? Do they know what their motivators are and how can they be leveraged? What changes in his or her work content, setting, or other variables could be integrated into his or her development goals and daily work life? Play an active role in helping to create a *context* that sets the stage for your organization's performer to succeed.

Remove obstacles to success. Your job as coach is to clear the decks so that the individual can develop their most critical skills. It is also a vote of confidence if you articulate your willingness to help provide the right resources. You may not have the authority to provide them directly, but you can work to influence others to secure them on the individual's behalf.

Provide perspectives on the organization that your employee can't possibly see from his or her position. It's a simple organizational truth: some things can only be seen from sufficient height or distance. An important element of coaching is offering that perspective by simply communicating good information: helping the individual see the organization in new, more complete ways so that he or she discovers new alternatives or strategies. That's true development.

A final note about learning from athletes: in sports, dance, and theater, coaches are often tough on their performers, but they never stop believing in them. In the Olympic study, they found that high expectations and a dedication to challenging the employee, the athlete, and the performer to develop their strengths to the maximum ability are key to their development.

> *When you focus on other people's shortcomings, they lose confidence in their abilities. But if you focus on their hard work and successes, you produce a sustainable increase in their self-confidence. What's more, researchers have discovered that the earlier in life you focus on a person's daily successes, the greater the gains over time.*
>
> — Tom Rath (2015)

Coaching and Mentoring in Education

The blend of mentoring and coaching relies on thoughtful teaching, what can be called *cognitive coaching*. Our field research explored the idea that the most effective professors or teachers are cognitive coaches. Are professors and teachers more effective if they view themselves and act as cognitive coaches? Jose Bowen, president of Goucher College thinks so (as cited in Young, 2017). The best teachers have more in common with fitness instructors, he argues. They motivate and guide their students to accomplish their goals.

We are in the midst of a paradigm shift from teaching to learning, from the "sage on the stage to the guide on the side." We now understand much more about how the brain works and how learning works. As Terry Doyle says, "The one who does the work, does the learning." (Doyle, 2011) So, as a teacher, we cannot do the work for you. The coachee, the student, the mentee has to do the work. A fitness coach can't exercise for you: only you can do that.

One of our authors recounts the experiences she had in graduate school with her dissertation advisor, Dr. Thomas M. Carsey.

Cognitive Coaching and Mentoring in Education

Paying It Forward
The first year of graduate school can be completely overwhelming. You're on a new campus surrounded by new students (who may or may not be competing with you for scholarships) and new faculty (who may only value you as long as you're teaching their courses). Lucky me — I got to do my first year of graduate school — twice!

I began a Ph.D. program at Texas A&M University only to have my advisor take a new job at a university in another state during my first year of the program. Unable to find another professor in the department whose research interests aligned with mine, I transferred to the University of North Carolina at Chapel Hill and repeated my first year of graduate school. This time around, I hoped to find a mentor who'd guide me throughout my entire grad school journey and beyond, whose behaviors

I could model, who would provide constructive advice, and who would support my personal and professional development — a professor who demonstrated the skills of a catalytic leader and who could be a valued mentor.

As he sauntered through the classroom door for a statistics lecture, in his dad jeans, braided belt, and faded t-shirt, I had no idea that Tom Carsey would become exactly that kind of mentor to me.

While grad school is intimidating, statistics classes and professors can be absolutely terrifying! But Tom knew how to make complicated lessons easy to grasp. He also knew how to infuse humor into scary situations to make them less intense.

For example, one day in stats class, Tom decided to tell us a story about his daughter, Jane, who was in elementary school at the time. He advised, "Don't let learning statistics scare you or the political science profession in general. Whenever my daughter Jane introduces me to her friends, she says, 'This is my daddy. He's a doctor!' But then she quickly adds, 'But not the kind that **helps** people.'" We all had a good laugh at that punchline. If Tom didn't take himself too seriously, we didn't have to either. He built an easy camaraderie; he clearly had our best interests in mind, and he was quick to offer his support as a trusted advisor and mentor.

Although Tom Carsey might not be the type of doctor people automatically think of when they think of helping people, he's spent his career becoming the type of professor who gives much more than he takes.

In the "publish-or-perish" world of higher education, it's not uncommon for faculty members to be far more concerned with their own research outputs than with their inputs into the lives of their colleagues or students. It's the rare faculty member who goes against the grain, devoting time, talent, and treasure to serve his or her colleagues, graduate students, and the department as a whole.

Luckily for students like me in the Department of Political Science, we know exactly what that unique type of professor looks like. Dr. Carsey is one of those rare professors willing to focus on others instead of himself and to pass along the knowledge and techniques he's developed over the course of his career to support the development of others.

When reflecting on the lessons she learned from Dr. Carsey, her Ph.D. advisor, that she'd like to pass along to her own students, Kristin Garrett, assistant professor at Wheaton College, quickly noted three things (personal communication, 2017):

1. Be a team player. Put the interests of others above yourself.

2. You can pursue and achieve excellence in your field and still invest powerfully in people.

3. Pay it forward by helping to challenge, encourage, and equip the next generation of students — because that's what my advisor did for me.

When asked why he devotes so much time and effort to mentoring graduate students, Carsey says, "I'm very proud of all of my students. My graduate advisors at Indiana University took the time to mentor me and give me the attention I needed to learn and develop in the discipline. I'm just *paying it forward*." (personal communication, 2017)

CONCLUSION

As Bacon and Voss point out in *Adaptive Coaching: The Art of Practice of a Client-Centered Approach to Performance Improvement*, "To coach effectively you must be adaptive. ...Find the right starting point on the infinite loop and then move fluidly from one perspective to another as the situation suggests... remember that clients possess greater wisdom about themselves and greater insight into what they can change and what, in their hearts, they know they cannot...support them on a journey that will always and inevitably be their own." (p. 317)

In order to fully understand the perspective of the individual you are mentoring or coaching, you must suspend your inclination to teach and instead become a master of asking questions. If you remember Detective Colombo from the TV series, he had a unique way of asking questions in order to get to the heart of the matter at hand.

Be curious like Colombo. Ask:

- How does that work?

- Do you think they'll go along with that? I'm really curious about why they would. What's in it for them?

- Why would you approach it *this* way rather than *that* way?

- Help me understand that. (This and the next statement are better than asking *Why?* because they don't sound challenging or evaluative.)

- I don't understand. *Or,* What I don't understand is why (this situation) is true (or not true). Help me out with that.

- Please explain. *Or,* Tell me more about (the situation or problem).

Although not all competencies are dependent on the presence of others, this one obviously is. To have maximum impact, this competency relies on having mastered earlier competencies. The two competencies, from among the 10 we have already described, that show up as predictors of effective mentoring relationships are your ability to connect emotionally and your ability to engender trust from others (Chun et al., 2010).

Take a moment to reflect on your own behavior, do you:

- Develop a shared understanding of ground rules for interactions?

- Develop a shared understanding of objectives and outcomes?

- Attempt to solve the individual's problems or do you lead them to the path of discovering their own answers?

- Appropriately advocate for the individual to members of the organization?

- Practice the art of asking good questions?

- Encourage individuals to experiment with new behaviors or approaches? Ensure the new behaviors have a powerful impact or ripple effect on the team or organization?

- Celebrate progress?

12

PROPOSES IMAGINATIVE SOLUTIONS

Definition: Presents creative, imaginative, and value-adding ideas for solving problems and achieving objectives.

Counter Behaviors: Rigid, advocates conventional approaches, resists experimenting with new ideas, resists change.

CATALYTIC COMPETENCIES MASTERED

Hank, an interviewee, is the MVP of the department, or in this instance, the MVE (Most Valuable *Engineer*): he has mastered many of the Catalyst Effect competencies early in his career. Team leaders seek out Hank to be a part of their projects. He brings to the team an ability to engage positively with everyone; understands and focuses on the overall team objectives; displays deep technical knowledge; and approaches problems with a seldom-seen level of curiosity and imagination (personal communication, 2017).

Although he has been with the civil engineering firm for only four years, he is the most sought-after catalytic team member out of dozens of engineers who are available for project work. His most recent project included surveying the site and establishing the building layout for a new bank branch at a high-visibility, high-volume intersection. The utility and traffic issues presented unique challenges to his team. Using the latest Real-Time Kinematic technology he was able to cut the number of days for project completion by 15%, delivering nearly perfect solutions to the customer ahead of schedule. The innovative nature of his solutions and the speed of the project's completion were noticed by the entire company, and to be sure, by the very satisfied client as well!

Project team managers fought over Hank in staff meetings; they wanted him on their team. Why? Because he added the most value to the team, not only by being an all-around pleasant guy to work with but also because even at his young age, he consistently offered innovative and creative ideas that bred solutions to complex problems. He was candidly curious and probed new ideas with an enthusiasm that few others brought to the table. This curiosity was built on an exceptionally strong set of engineering skills honed at one of the top universities in the country and through a series of internships with top firms.

In our conversations with both Hank and his group manager, they demurred that this feeding frenzy over Hank resulted in a combination of both amusement and pride. How could project managers make such a big fuss over having him, this young kid, on their team rather than any number of other more experienced engineers in the organization? We discovered that the primary driver was his ability to view situations with a fresh perspective — to offer creative ideas in an energetic manner that piqued the interest of others. Not only did this young man have "the whole package" of personal and team skills addressed in the first 11 competencies, but he also punched above his weight and contributed beyond his experience offering innovative ideas to problems that seemed quite routine in the field. He was bold and unabashedly curious. He noted that his favorite questions included: "Why are we doing it this way?" "I see it differently; can we look at it from a different angle for a minute?" "This may be a dumb question, but let me ask it anyway...?"

How was he able to apply this level of imagination and creativity so early in his career?

As the authors spoke with Hank, he was modest in describing his success. He attributed his near-celebrity status in the organization to several impactful experiences and development opportunities. His family background provided him with a commonsense approach to problem-solving of all types. As a family who was in business for themselves, everyone worked hard, pitched in on whatever needed to be done, and solved problems on their own whenever they could. His parents always valued his ideas and curiosity. His hometown provided opportunities for him to serve on the town's mayoral advisory group as a student member. He learned about real issues and the imperative of finding practical solutions quickly.

The early development of these catalytic competencies obviously served him well as a young professional, and he ultimately earned a seat at the table with more seasoned engineers. He's an excellent example of an individual having a catalytic impact early in his career.

SPURRING CREATIVE IDEAS

Have you considered where or how you get your most imaginative and impactful ideas? Does your work environment give you the freedom to actively explore novel ideas? How do you and your teammates support each other's curiosity regarding challenges and opportunities?

Let's examine the views of well-known researcher and author Clay Christensen (2016). He builds his view of innovation around the belief that new ideas do not usually emerge from a single person or function. They are sparked by interactions among people who have never met before or function where they have not previously worked together.

They may transform how we accomplish tasks, deliver services, and live our lives — making former ways obsolete. The marketplace generally decides. This is often referred to as *creative destruction*. But you can also think of it as *creative construction* — discovering or inventing and applying novel ways of achieving objectives and getting others to adopt them. *Great catalysts do that in big and small ways — their incremental imaginative proposals are as transforming as major breakthroughs.*

Christensen's view of creative destruction evolved to a more integrated perspective as to how consumers drive innovation, what he describes as *jobs theory*. Its principles are surprisingly simple. Innovators focus on the underlying aspects of a potential customer's *job*, the way in which he or she is trying to make progress in certain circumstances. The unique view that Christensen brings is that the company's offering can be recast as something customers "hire" or bring into their lives to make progress on the topic of interest. This serves to focus the innovative work on *why* they do it, not the customer themselves as the target.

> *Jobs theory essentially transforms products into services.*
> — Christensen, 2016

In Christensen's model, he explores, "What causes a customer to purchase and use a particular product or service?" For example, OnStar evolved from a collection of nifty features to an integrated communications system for the car. But it really took off when developers defined the customer's job as to attain peace of mind when he or she is driving. Ikea is another example. The company doesn't target any specific demographic; rather, customers hire the company to "help me furnish my apartment today." (Christensen, 2016)

When an employee takes a coffee break, they are hiring a beverage for the emotional benefit of relaxing or taking a mental break. Any beverage will do if the activity provides them with an opportunity to chat with their friends. For many, Facebook has become the universal coffee break. It is an innovation that has changed users social interactions across demographics.

Jobs theory essentially transforms products into services. "What matters is not the product attributes you rope together, but the experiences you enable to help your customers make the progress they want to make," the authors write (Christensen, 2016). To foster a creative mind-set, Christensen suggests that jobs are discovered, not created by active minds in search of new ideas. He suggests that there are opportunities for innovation wherever intersections of multiple needs occur, such as Open Table's juggling multiple guests and restaurant choices with varying availability. The service or job that many have learned to use and love is the walk-in clinic at CVS. It is typically filled with families, especially kids, who need to address a relatively routine medical issue with an efficient, quality solution.

Christensen has been uncovering additional successful companies that have deployed a version of this approach. In the most successful cases, brands have become identified with the jobs customers have hired them to do. Examples include Intuit, Match.com, Keurig, Disney, and FedEx.

> Innovation takes many forms. Regardless of the nuances, a faster pace of change requires more ideas and more innovative initiatives in order to keep up.

THE THREE-PART PATTERN OF IMAGINATIVE SOLUTIONS

Historic innovations lend insight into how effective catalysts generate breakthrough or transformative ideas. Let's take a quick look back.

The invention of the printing press in the 1400s was driven by three interconnected factors and an integrative pattern of thinking: the need for less expensive and time-consuming production of printed material (solution need), **plus** combining acquired expertise with existing knowledge, **plus** experimentation and testing to create new technology.

Variations of this three-part pattern (recognition of a need for a solution plus connecting newly acquired knowledge, outside observations, existing know-how, or trends plus experimentation and application to new uses) shows up time and again throughout history for the creation of transformative innovations.

This invention pattern repeats for the electric light, telegraph, electronic calculator, personal computer, smartphone, sports analytics, the creation of new music by Yo-Yo Ma and the Silk Road Ensemble, and many more. A modern cutting-edge demonstration of this pattern, with a catalytic team twist, can also be found in the best practices of Onyx Solar and the development of photovoltaic glass.

Photovoltaic transparent glass technology efficiently converts light into electricity, enabling insulating glass panels to be integrated into the architectural design of new or existing buildings — such as sky lights, regular windows, and window walls — eliminating the need for roof-mounted solar panels and producing a swift return on investment. Onyx Solar is a leader in this field (Onyx Solar, n.d.a). Their innovation springs from a continual search for practical innovative ideas coupled with research and development investments. Their catalytic momentum often originates with their "Committee of Wise People," who are continuously developing and proposing novel solutions to meet green energy challenges (Onyx Solar, n.d.b). As the company's website (http://www.onyxsolar.com/wisemen.html, 2017) explains, this catalytic team "combine(s) forces in research, design and development of Building Integrated Photovoltaic solutions." The team includes architects, engineers, and scientists focused on:

- "Supporting global green building market expansion.

- Helping to create and provide more green building resources for industry professionals around the world.

- Increasing project and firm-level intelligence to help faster market growth."

Onyx Solar's process for creating novel solutions largely parallels those of historic breakthrough innovations.

The Three-Part Pattern involves:

1. Recognizing the need for cost-effective, non-add-on (architecturally integrated) solar energy panels (a market-attractive solution need).

2. Connecting acquired and developed multifunctional expertise with existing knowledge.

3. Leveraging and applying existing science to create new technology.

Onyx Solar's "Committee of Wise People" enabled them to efficiently pursue multidisciplinary concepts and transcend functional boundaries. By combining and integrating ideas, bringing in outside perspectives, and proposing how technologies developed elsewhere can be integrated or applied, this team gave Onyx greater ability to catalytically innovate, which in turn led to the development of leading-edge products that propelled and sustained marketplace competitiveness.

> *Teams working on disruptive ideas need to be small enough that they can be fed by no more than two pizzas.*
>
> — Scott Anthony (2011)

Wise People Committees

One way catalysts develop imaginative solutions is by bringing people with different expertise together to combine and integrate ideas for meeting current and emerging challenges. In this regard, all teams can learn from Onyx's playbook. Powerful catalytic ideas are sparked by an open-thinking process and a team of people with different areas of expertise, perspectives, insights, and ideas who focus on creating innovative breakthroughs. These may be big creative ideas with the potential to catapult success or incremental improvements that build on one another—sometimes referred to as continuous improvement. Both can be transforming in different ways and propel catalytic performance.

IMAGINATIVE IDEAS IN PRACTICE: WHAT YOU CAN DO TO ACTIVATE CREATIVITY

How do imaginative ideas originate? Not solely from "eureka" moments. Epiphanies, when they occur, often follow from a series of human and mental connections, including the following.

Connections with the Expertise of Others Are Key

Engagement with others, especially those with different knowledge sets or ways of thinking, is often a powerful way of generating new ideas. This is particularly likely when ideas and insights are developed judgment-free as with pure brainstorming. Geniuses like Thomas Edison did not develop most of their ideas and invent new devices huddled alone in a lab. Edison assembled a team of scientists and engineers who worked by his side. It was through their interactions and combination of expertise that breakthroughs like the cotton gin and kinetoscope (motion picture viewer) were invented (Hughes, 2014). Teams that openly bounce around perspectives, insights, and ideas for how to address a challenge are generally more adept at developing novel solutions than people working alone.

Connections with Outside/Non-Job Phenomena Make a Difference

Allowing the mind to wander while considering the world around you can create serendipitous mental connections. Exposure to outside stimuli that may have, on the surface, little or nothing to do with challenges you wish to tackle, may precipitate conceptual leaps. For example, a busy anthill may elicit ideas about teamwork, communication, or construction. Or hydrophonic microphones may stimulate a new piece of music based on under-sea communication among blue whales. Commenting on creative ideas, Drake Baer in a post on *Business Insider* notes that the spark that allows us to come up with new ideas is usually an analogy: a way of looking at two things in your memory or in the world and seeing the similarity in their underlying structures (Hughes, 2014). Making analogous connections triggers imaginative ideas because they compel our minds to see things in a different light. Often those connections come at unexpected times, in unpredictable ways, and from unplanned events.

Connections with Experience and Existing Knowledge

Knowledge by itself is only a starting point in developing imaginative solutions. Knowledge must be connected with experiences, past and present. Certainly, Steve Jobs, founder of Apple Computer, was one of the innovative giants of our time. He commented, "Creativity is just connecting things. When you ask creative people how they did something, they feel a little guilty because they didn't really do it, they just saw something." (cited in Wolf, 1996) In actual practice, they saw something and linked it with something they had already experienced or learned. Jobs goes on to explain that they "were able to connect experiences they've had and synthesize new things. And the reason they were able to do that was that they simply have had more experiences than other people." (cited in Wolf, 1996) More experiences lead to greater knowledge upon which to draw — and the ability to make connections that in turn lead to development of creative solutions.

Connections with Trends

New trends are constantly emerging. Some are fleeting. Others take flight and alter the business and competitive landscape for years, if not permanently. When paradigms shift, alert catalysts shift with them and build upon them. If they don't, the health of their endeavors is jeopardized, and aspirations are dashed. In the arts, The Beatles are a great example of a *team* that spotted trends in music, politics, and the habits and interests of their audiences. They not only kept pace with these trends, but they also helped shape them through their imaginative studio productions, lyrics, and melodies. They were among the first to see the trend in synthesized music and experimented with it continuously. They led the trend away from pop music reflected in their early songs to socially conscious recordings, creating sounds and lyrics that resonated with the counter cultural movement of the times. They not only changed with their audience, but they also stayed a step ahead of it.

> *Powerful new ideas often come from combining old concepts, solutions, or methods that ignite a proven process with fresh ideas and technological advances. Sometimes they disrupt entire industries.*

COMPLACENCY IS DANGEROUS

Complacency based on past innovation is dangerous. Vigilant catalysts avoid this trap and help keep their organizations and teams on the leading edge. Dartmouth business professor Vijay Govindarajan, coauthor of *The Other Side of Innovation* explains, "Successful companies tend to fall into [three traps]…that make the glory days fleeting. First is the physical trap, in which big investments in old systems or equipment prevent the pursuit of fresher, more relevant investments. There's a psychological trap, in which company leaders fixate on what made them successful and fail to notice when something new is displacing it. Then there's the strategic trap, when a company focuses purely on the marketplace of today and fails to anticipate the future." (cited in Newman, 2010)

Catalysts help organizations steer clear of these traps and break free of entrenched patterns, complacency or inertia, and obsolete ways of thinking. They do this by repeatedly making connections — connections with the expertise of others, connections with outside phenomena, connections with prior knowledge and experience, and connections with emerging or new trends — and using them as springboards for developing novel ideas to propel future success.

Cultivating Your Ability to Develop Imaginative Solutions

There are relatively well-defined criteria for predicting *who* will generate creative ideas as Tomas Chamorro-Premuzic explains in *The Talent Delusion* (2017). He maintains that some people are disproportionately more likely to come up with novel and useful ideas. Regardless of their field of expertise, job title, and occupational background, creative individuals display a recurrent set of psychological characteristics and behaviors. Creative people tend to be better at identifying (rather than solving) problems, they are passionate and sensitive, and, above all, they tend to have a hungry mind: they are open to new experiences, nonconformist, and curious. He cites the findings of more than 100 studies that indicate personality characteristics as stronger determinants of creative potential than IQ, school performance, or motivation.

Creativity alone, however, is not sufficient for innovation: innovation also requires the development, production, and implementation of an idea. As we noted earlier in this chapter, creativity is the ability to identify and develop imaginative ideas; innovation is the deployment of the idea into action. The following are among the characteristics Chamorro-Premuzic (2017) describes as key:

1. An opportunistic mind-set that helps them identify gaps in the market.

2. Proactivity and a high degree of persistence, which enable them to exploit the opportunities they identify.

3. A healthy dose of prudence. Contrary to what many people think, successful innovators are organized, cautious, and weigh risks carefully.

4. Social capital. Serial innovators tend to use their connections and networks to mobilize resources and build strong alliances, both internally and externally.

These four characteristics are necessary, but not sufficient. Imaginative ideas and innovative implementation are unlikely to occur in the absence of additional factors: passion for the mission of the organization and a longer term vision of team success. As a highly impactful catalyst on your team, you must not only be creative, opportunistic, or proactive, but you must also have the ability to propel others toward the implementation of new ideas — innovation.

The culture that you foster on your teams can ensure that you remain innovative even when you have experienced substantial success. Rather than falling into the trap of complacency when the new idea is working well, the role of the catalyst is to curiously poke, prod, and press for opportunities to improve on what may be working already.

In short, there is no point in just hoping for a breakthrough idea — what matters is the ability to generate *many* ideas, discover the right opportunities to develop them, and act with drive and dedication to achieve a meaningful goal. Ideas don't make people successful — it's the other way around.

In my mind, so-called 'cultures of innovation' really boil down to one word: curiosity.

— Scott D. Anthony (2011)

CONCLUSION

In the opening story in this chapter, the young engineer Hank was a sought-after catalyst for project teams. He displayed many or most of the competencies described in the first 11 chapters of the book, and in addition, he was an imaginative thinker. He brought an energetic curiosity to the team that ignited creativity. *Are you, like Hank, a sought-after catalytic team member?*

Catalysts pay attention to trends and make connections with past experiences, their knowledge base, their values, and their passions to forge new paths forward. They constantly pursue connections and exchange insights with a wide range of people with diverse experience and knowledge, connect problems with independent analogous observations, and make links with current challenges. They continuously seek new experiences. They let their mind wander, especially at relaxed moments, to make conceptual connections. They jot down their observations and thoughts, review them, and look for relationships to arrive at imaginative conclusions.

Bestselling author and thought leader Gary Hamel (n.d.) writes, "Innovation starts with the heart — with a passion for improving the lives of those around you." Catalysts, in essence, must have a passion for benefiting and making significant differences in the lives of others through their creativity, ingenuity, and hard work. Hamel goes on to proclaim: "The best innovations — both socially and economically — come from the pursuit of ideals that are noble and timeless: joy, wisdom, beauty, truth, equality, community, sustainability and love. These are the things we live for, and the innovations that really make a difference are the ones that are life enhancing. And that's why the heart of innovation is a desire to re-enchant the world." (n.d.)

Catalysts pursue noble goals connected to elevating the performance of their coworkers, teams, and organization. They seek to make a positive difference and meaningfully enhance lives — and mobilize those who work with them to do the same. They endeavor to do so from wherever they are — as a team member, individual contributor, manager, or from whatever position they may be in.

Catalytic leadership comes from within and is expressed through applying the 12 catalytic competencies in the four cornerstones:

1. **Building Credibility** is necessary for imaginative ideas to take flight. The proposer needs to be trusted, be able to communicate clearly and connect the ideas to benefits and objectives, and rally others or invigorate with their optimistic beliefs and passion.

2. **Creating Cohesion** must be built through development of strong relationships, camaraderie, emotional connections, and a track record for putting the team's goals ahead of personal interests.

3. **Generating Momentum** is generated by energizing others to execute with the mission in mind, upgrading and rejuvenating capabilities to be continuously successful, and following the lead of others when their expertise is most relevant for the tasks at hand.

4. **Amplifying Impact** is achieved through pursuit of excellence, mentoring and coaching others, and proposing imaginative solutions to challenges big and small, tactical and strategic.

Take a moment to reflect on your own behavior, do you:

- **Engage in daily activities that activate your mind** in different ways — from physical exercise to intellectual stimulation to music? Deeply connect with your environment and explore new places that stretch your boundaries?

- **Imagine success?** Paint a picture in your mind of what success in creatively solving a problem or achieving a goal looks like. Make it vivid. Describe what people will be doing or feeling once results are achieved. Illustrate graphically what incredible success will look like. Then plot the steps for bringing it about. "What if we are wildly successful?" Imagine it.

- **Deepen and expand what you know and can do?** Dive into new subjects and develop greater expertise in your own field. Think about connections between what you already know, what you are learning, and how the combination can help lead to new ideas and ways of meeting challenges.

- **Make curiosity a passion?** Be inquisitive. Look for options outside of what is familiar to you by examining how things are done in wildly disparate industries or places. Ask questions like "Why do you recommend doing it _____ way instead of _____ way? What are the benefits? What are the pitfalls? What mistakes did you make and what did you learn from them?

- **Brainstorm: Springboard off the expertise and insights of others?** Brainstorm with others to inspire fresh ideas. Brainstorm with a variety of people and groups, including those beyond your normal circle. Take the initiative to assemble diverse groups that you think could produce creative ideas. Note all ideas, no matter how crazy or unrealistic they may seem.

Sometimes there is a valuable kernel inside them. Often they build on the ideas you hear. Merge potential approaches into a potential remedy. Think fluidly and flexibly and ask others to do the same.

- **Join or form ideation sessions inside or outside of work?** Ideation is an engaging process for generating and conveying imaginative ideas, while brainstorming usually focuses on an existing challenge. Ideation is more about future possibilities — describing what could be, sometimes building on what exists and at other times starting with a clean slate. It is more aspirational and visionary.

WHAT'S NEXT?
ASSESSING AND DEVELOPING
CATALYTIC COMPETENCIES

Several years ago, Henry Mintzberg (2005) wrote a book assailing business schools called *Managers Not MBAs*. The 21st-century version might be, "Catalysts Not Managers."

— Bill Fanelli, personal communication, 2014

What's next, if you aspire to develop the competencies needed to become a catalytic teammate and leader?

As we've highlighted in the preceding 12 chapters, the behaviors required to improve on each competency can be developed. We suggested specific steps you might take to impact each. Specific behaviors that underlie each can be developed through

1. Cognitive understanding of what needs to be done.

2. Drive and commitment to improve.

3. Implementation of practices described in the preceding 12 competency chapters.

You may recall the introductory story in Chapter 9 ("Leads and Follows") in which Beth, the symphony vice president-turned improv player, learned to be outgoing and social by experimenting with new skills as a young girl. She attacked her shyness by playing a role and trying new behaviors that dramatically improved her communication skills. She and her friend understood what they wanted to achieve, they possessed the drive and motivation to go after it, and they employed new practices in order to develop the desired competencies.

Even as an accomplished communicator and platform speaker today, she continues to hone her platform skills by pushing herself to be uncomfortable on the improv stage, placing herself in situations that require her to test and develop her skills. She allows herself to be vulnerable as she tries new things in order to improve.

Are you willing to commit to development as strongly and specifically as Beth has? It's important to not only commit to making improvements in certain areas but also put ourselves in situations where we can take the risks, expose ourselves, be open to floundering a bit the first time or two around as we try new catalytic behaviors.

> *Don't focus on what someone can't do and complain about it.*
> *Focus on what they can do and help them get the most out of it.*
> — Brad Stevens, Head Coach,
> Boston Celtics (Duckworth, 2016)

Of course, if there is little motivation to improve, then little will change. If the person truly does not care about the team, then putting the team first is not a "training" challenge at all.

Significant personal change may mean that the work you need to put into the effort will likely feel like, well, work. Sports psychologist James Taylor (2015) calls this junction *The Grind*, which starts when actions necessary to produce meaningful change become stressful and tedious, especially if there is no immediate, visible progress toward the goal.

The Grind is also the point at which your efforts toward change really count. It is what separates those who are able to make significant changes from those who are not. Many people who reach this point in the process of change either ease up or quit because it is just too darned hard. As we mentioned in Chapter 10, being committed to doing The Hard Thing and be willing to keep after it through The Grind is essential. If mastery of a complex skill requires 10,000 hours of dedicated practice, then yes, mastering new catalytic skills will require some work as well.

> *Confidence is what happens when you've done the hard work that*
> *entitles you to succeed.*
> — Pat Summitt, former Head Basketball Coach,
> University of Tennessee, Lady Vols (2012)

HOW CATALYTIC ARE YOU?

Here are three steps with assessment and planning tools for evaluating your level of catalytic behavior and launching next steps.

Step 1: Assess Yourself

The following is a series of statements, each presented in pairs (see next page). Each pair represents two ends of a continuum. Read each pair of statements. Then decide whether the statement on the left or the statement on the right best describes you.

Step Two: Score Your Self-Assessment

To determine how catalytic you are, add up the points in the boxes you circled. The highest score possible is 84 (extremely catalytic) and the lowest score possible is 7 (not at all catalytic). Record your overall Catalyst score here: _____

As you learned in reading the book, there are four cornerstones that underpin the Catalyst Effect: Building Credibility, Creating Cohesion, Generating Momentum, and Amplifying Impact.

To determine how catalytic you are in each of these cornerstone areas, fill in the blanks below:

1. **Building Credibility**: Add your scores for statements #1−3 together (max = 21, min = 3) = ____

2. **Creating Cohesion**: Add your scores for statements #4−6 together (max = 21, min = 3) = ____

3. **Generating Momentum**: Add your scores for statements #7−9 together (max = 21, min = 3) = ____

4. **Amplifying Impact**: Add your scores for statements #10−12 together (max = 21, min = 3) = ____

Your scores in each of the four Cornerstones enable you to begin to identify areas where you may have developmental opportunities!

	Statement on the left *strongly* describes me.	Statement on the left *mostly* describes me.	Statement on the left *somewhat* describes me.	*In the middle or both* describe me equally.	Statement on the right *somewhat* describes me.	Statement on the right *mostly* describes me.	Statement on the right *strongly* describes me.	
Competency #1 *I do everything I can to live authentically. I regularly demonstrate ethical principles in a manner that promotes trust.*	7	6	5	4	3	2	1	*Sometimes I skew the facts of a situation and create a biased impression. I don't always say what I'm thinking or present myself as I truly am.*
Competency #2 *Sometimes I fail to pay attention to what others are saying and communicate my ideas in an unclear manner.*	1	2	3	4	5	6	7	*I consciously attempt to speak and write clear and concise messages and to listen closely for understanding.*

Competency #3 I energize others with a confident, hope-filled outlook. I convey a "can-do" attitude.	7	6	5	4	3	2	1	I tend to critique new ideas and may unintentionally deflate the energy and optimism of others.
Competency #4 I'm not very concerned about others' emotional reactions and am reluctant to acknowledge how they are feeling.	1	2	3	4	5	6	7	I read the emotional signals of others accurately and respond appropriately to them.
Competency #5 I fit in naturally with others and regularly foster positive interactions.	7	6	5	4	3	2	1	I frequently have a hard time connecting and interacting with others.
Competency #6 I do less than I could to achieve results and occasionally lose sight of big picture goals.	1	2	3	4	5	6	7	I prioritize team success and processes over my own personal goals and I do whatever it takes to achieve results and pursue overarching organizational goals.

(Continued)

	Statement on the left *strongly* describes me.	Statement on the left *mostly* describes me.	Statement on the left *somewhat* describes me.	*In the middle or both* describe me equally.	Statement on the right *somewhat* describes me.	Statement on the right *mostly* describes me.	Statement on the right *strongly* describes me.	
Competency #7 I do whatever I can to elevate the performance of others and my team as a whole.	7	6	5	4	3	2	1	I generally focus on how well I'm doing personally, rather than on how I'm contributing to the success of the team or how others are performing.
Competency #8 I'm generally satisfied with my current skill set and level of knowledge and don't actively pursue suggestions and opportunities for improvement.	1	2	3	4	5	6	7	I'm a highly curious person and actively pursue personal and professional improvement opportunities.

Competency	1	2	3	4	5	6	7	
Competency #9 I recognize and respect the knowledge and skills of others and seek to learn from them.	7	6	5	4	3	2	1	I drive to do things my own way and tend to resist the recommendations of others.
Competency #10 My knowledge and expertise are not as advanced as many others in our organization and I don't press others to improve.	1	2	3	4	5	6	7	I possess extensive knowledge and/or competence and encourage others to develop the same attributes.
Competency #11 I model exemplary behavior and actively support the personal and professional development of others.	7	6	5	4	3	2	1	I don't worry much about how others see me and rarely work with others to help them improve.
Competency #12 I generally recommend traditional solutions to problems and shy away from risky new ideas.	1	2	3	4	5	6	7	I present creative, novel, and valuable ideas for achieving objectives and solving problems.

Step Three: Determine Current Strengths and Areas for Improvement within each of the 12 Competencies

At the end of every chapter, we provided a list of suggestions for applying and developing each competency. For example, at the end of Chapter 1, "Acts with Integrity and Inspires Trust," the following checklist was provided:

- Live your values consistently.
- Align intentions with the greater good.
- Keep personal ego and ambition in check.
- Keep commitments and promises.
- Act and speak honestly.
- Act authentically.

We invited you to note the behaviors on the list that you felt you were already doing well and to circle the items where you felt you had room to improve. In this section, you'll record your strengths and areas for improvement. In the next section, you'll create action plans to become more catalytic.

Let's Get Started

To fill in the grid below, you may want to return to the conclusion of each of the 12 competency chapters. You may want to start with the competencies that are part of the cornerstone on which you rated yourself the lowest, that is, where you have the most opportunity to improve. If you didn't review the checklist at the end of each chapter as you read through the book, take some time now to review those before attempting to fill in the grid below. Note: We have provided a sample grid for Chapter 1, Competency #1 below. Rather than repeating this grid for each of the other 11 competencies, we invite you to copy it, or download a template from our website, www.catalysteffect.org. This will enable you to record the action steps that you identify for each competency.

Instructions

Review the suggested action steps for each competency. For each action step, put a check in the "I currently do this" column if you feel like that is a strength of yours. If it's not a strength yet, put a check in the "I can improve in this area" column.

	Practices	I Currently Do This. It Is a Strength	I Can Improve in This Area	Actions I Will Take to Bolster a Strength; or to Improve
Competency 1 *Acts with Integrity and Inspires Trust*	Live your values consistently.			
	Align intentions with the greater good.			
	Keep personal ego and ambition in check.			
	Keep commitments and promises.			
	Act and speak honestly.			
	Act authentically.			
Note: Blank row for the reader to copy.... **Separate from the box above ??**	**Add headings for the blank copy....**			

After you've determined which practices are your strengths and areas for improvement, identify three to four actions you can take for each to:

1) Further boost each strength.

2) Improve in those areas you have identified.

List them in the appropriate boxes in the far right column in the table above. A partial list of suggested development activities can be found at the end of each chapter. Inside each chapter are many more. Refer to them for ideas.

As you launch your catalytic action plan, we recommend selecting a manageable number of activities as starting points. Choose those that you believe should be your top priorities. Then, as you develop proficiency in them, add others on your list, and refer to the book for additional suggestions. You may want to review your action activities list on a regular basis and use it as a reminder.

With your self-rating and the input from others' in mind, identify your "strongest three" — those which you can continue to build and utilize effectively; and the three that need the most improvement, that is your "weakest three." For your strongest, identify specific ways you can use these skills on your team. For the three in most need of development, analyze the nature of the gap between your current and desired behavior. Identify the specific verbal, nonverbal behaviors that you need to change or learn to close the gap. Drive for actionable steps to improve and be specific versus being generally descriptive.

For example, if you want to improve the competency *Communicates Clearly*, a general behavioral goal might be "strive to listen more carefully." But that is not very measurable and implies only effort, not a specific behavior and resulting impact (the other person experiences being listened to).

A more specific goal would be as follows: "talk 30–50% less, leaving clear openings and air time for the other person to speak; then paraphrase what I heard them say." If your relationship with the other person is comfortable enough, follow up with a checkpoint at the end of the conversation: "Did you feel like I understood what you were saying, and why?"

> *Good players want to be coached. Great players want to be told the truth.*
>
> — Doc Rivers, quoted by @Coaching U (January 23, 2015)

HOW YOU WORK BEST WITH OTHERS: A SELF-REFLECTION IN PRACTICE

How do you have a catalytic effect on your team(s)? How can you describe your approach to leading/influencing to others, including your team, so that they understand more clearly how you work best with them... and they with you?

We find that few people can articulate an answer to these questions in a thoughtful, crisp manner. Many of us have not consolidated our thinking about how we impact the team and conversely, what working styles we prefer from others. The actions of others that bug or annoy us may be easy to identify. But in an interview, for example, few of us can begin our self-description as follows: "Here are three key aspects of my work style that positively influence the teams of which I am a member. Let me start by outlining them; and then I'd like to give you an example or two if you are interested."

We encourage you to be able to articulate a cogent statement as to how you influence and lead others. The following ideas may be helpful.

MBA students at Butler University are asked to explore three questions as one step in their development as catalytic leaders. With the support of faculty and a designated leadership coach, they explore their leadership and teamwork styles from three perspectives (cognitive, emotional, and behavioral):

- How do you *think* about leadership; what cognitive models or frameworks guide your thinking?

- How do you *feel* about leading and about working with others? What is your natural approach to interacting with others, and how have your life experiences impacted this style?

- How do you *behave* as a leader/team member? What do others see and experience when you are in the room? How do you visibly live out your values?

A CATALYTIC PERSPECTIVE

The sample narrative below addresses these questions from the perspective of a young professional woman, Landry, who is eager to grow.

During Landry's first meeting with the new team, she shares the following ideas about her working style and her career:

> I'm excited to be part of this team. I look forward to working with each of you and getting to know each of you better over the coming months. For the past year or so, I have had a sounding board, a coach/mentor if you will, who has encouraged me to think more deliberately about my work style. I've learned a ton about myself and have grown my confidence and my skills.
>
> This has not been easy. There have been some rough spots as I have addressed my competencies, my gaps, and the need to improve. But the process has been worth it, and I want to continue to grow, with your support and input.
>
> I realize that for our organization to achieve the best results, our teams must develop excellent working relationships. Without them we don't "win" together; work can end up being drudgery versus satisfying and fun. With that in mind, I'd like to share my thoughts about how I approach my work.
>
> You know a bit about my career at the company, e.g., what positions I have held and the key projects I have worked on, from staffing the call center in my first role here to the most recent project that focused on improving customer service. But you don't know me, and I don't know you at all when it comes to "why I approach my work, the way I do."
>
> When I started here I didn't have a clue as to how to work effectively on a team. I did not know myself very well at all and I did not know what was expected of me to be able to perform well on teams. Through a number of project experiences along with

team participation in recreational basketball, my relationship with my boyfriend and perhaps "just maturing" in general, I'm now able to define much more clearly how I can be effective. I know more about what to do and what not to do. It has built my confidence along with my comfort in sharing these ideas with you.

- *I'm not a very complicated person. I'm driven by common values, and I learned early on from my parents that "you don't tell a lie." Even when it came to the little things that my brother, sister and I fought about, honesty was an absolute rule. My relationships today are built on a similar value of honesty and reliable demonstration of that by others. I prefer to have direct conversations with others, even about potentially sensitive issues: I'd much rather hear about something early on than later, especially if there is an issue that is causing a problem...and especially if the issue might relate to something I am doing, or not doing. "No surprises" is my motto.*

- *I communicate best face-to-face, and one-to-one. So if we have something important to talk about, whether it is about a project, performance expectations, how we are working together... whatever it is...please let me know earlier rather than later. I prefer to set up time in advance to talk about key issues so I don't feel surprised or blindsided. My calendar is busy, but orderly. Some might say I'm a bit OCD when it comes to my schedule... I like working face-to-face versus on the phone or via email. And, as you know, I "really" like talking over coffee at the Roastery (hint, hint)!*

- *I try to be (realistically) optimistic. I've learned that building an agreement with others early on as to how we will be successful as a team is vital to achieving that success. I prefer clear, defined metrics. I expect the very best of you, and of the teams I am working on and I hope you expect my very best as well. I work hard at trying to see the glass as half full vs half empty; in finding things that are going well vs being the critic.*

- *The team comes first. When I find that people are not fully committed to our team's success, it's difficult for me to respect them and their work ethic. I try hard to build their commitment and focus on the payoffs for them individually and for the team. Yes, I'm here to achieve my personal goals and grow my career, but I know from experience that I am most satisfied when we win together. I regularly work 50–60 hours per week. I don't expect everyone else to do so, but if we are hard pressed to complete a project, I do expect that we each do whatever needs to be done. I know I spend too much time at work, but that is how I am built. My basketball teammates kid me about my floor burns as I dive for loose balls. My personal life suffers a bit from my work hours, but my boyfriend knows this, and we work it out. He gets on my calendar, eh?*

- *On the other hand, don't be surprised if I pop in unexpectedly and test a new idea with you! I do like the informal exchange of ideas. Please catch me in the hallway or anywhere...and I hope I can do the same...to offer up new ways of doing things even if they are crazy ideas at the time. I am working at getting better at these informal discussions.*

- *P.S. If I don't want to be interrupted at my work station, I have my "Ideas Percolating" sign up with the picture of the coffee pot, which means don't disturb me right now.*

- *Mentoring and coaching are important to me. I've had the benefit of having two terrific mentors in my career, as well as a professional coach for a few months last year. They have been terrific sounding boards and have encouraged me to address my "gaps" and to put a plan together to improve them and to recognize my strengths and celebrate them!*

- *I've found that I'm a pretty good informal leader of projects, for instance, and my confidence continues to grow in that regard. I've been here long enough that I can serve as a sounding board for newer folks about how to get things done. You have my promise that anything you tell me privately will be held in the strictest of confidence. If you ask me about your work or how you can improve, I'll share my honest views. Don't ask unless you really want to know. Bottom-line, I'm here to help us win together...and have fun doing so.*

I trust that you now have a better idea of what makes me tick... how I work...and what you can expect from me as a colleague. I'm not static and this self-reflection will change from time to time, I realize. But I trust that it provides a path to learning how we can best work with each other.

I look forward to learning more about you as well, so feel free set up some time for coffee and we'll talk!

Thanks!

You have just read Landry's perspective as to how she leads and how she believes she can be catalytic with others. As you reflect on your approach to leading from the middle or wherever you are in your organization, what would you say is a description of your style and approach?

Thank you for exploring leadership with us from a unique perspective. Join us at our website for catalytic updates, mini-cases, and other resources.

We wish you luck on your catalytic journey!

REFERENCES

A Great Place to Work (2016). *The business case for a high-trust culture.* Retrieved from https://s3.amazonaws.com/media.greatplacetowork.com/pdfs/Business+Case_Detailed+Report_Final.pdf

Abrams, L. C., Cross, R., Lesser, E., & Levin, D. (2003). Nurturing interpersonal trust in knowledge-sharing networks. *The Academy of Management Executive (1993–2005), 17*(4), 64–77. Retrieved from http://www.jstor.org/stable/4166007

Ackman, D. (2002). Billionaire secrets: Excellence sought — And found. *Forbes*, October 4. Retrieved from https://www.forbes.com/2002/10/04/1004excellent.html

Anthony, S. D. (2011). *The little black book of innovation: How it works, how to do it.* Boston, MA: Harvard Business Review Press.

Army Values. (n.d.). The soldier's creed. Retrieved from https://www.army.mil/values/soldiers.html

Avey, J. B., Luthans, F., & Wernsing, S. (2008). Can positive employees help positive organizational change? Impact of psychological capital and emotions on relevant attitudes and behaviors. *The Journal of Applied Behavioral Science, 44*(1), 48–70.

Avey, J. B., Reichard, R. J., Luthans, F., & Mhatre, K. H. (2011). Meta-analysis of the impact of positive psychological capital on employee attitudes, behaviors, and performance. *Human Resource Development Quarterly, 22*(2), 127–152.

Bachman, R. (2010). Tom Jernstedt, longtime boss of the NCAA Tournament, steps down. *The Oregonian*, August 16. Retrieved from http://www.oregonlive.com/sports/index.ssf/2010/08/tom_jernstedt_long-time_boss_of.html

Bandura, A. (1982). Self-efficacy mechanism in human agency. *American Psychologist*, 37, 122–147.

Barney, J. B., & Hansen, M. H. (1994). Trustworthiness as a source of competitive advantage. *Strategic Management Journal*, (15), 175–190.

Barsh, J., Capozzi, M. M., & Davidson, J. (2008). Leadership and innovation. *McKinsey Quarterly*, 1, 37–47.

Bersin, J. (2012). The new best-practices of a high-impact learning organization. *Bersin, by Deloitte*, September 4. Retrieved from http://blog.bersin.com/the-new-best-practices-of-a-high-impact-learning-organization/

Blake, R. R., & Mouton, J. S. (1994). *The managerial grid*. Houston, TX: Gulf Publishing.

Bollen, K. A., & Hoyle, R. H. (1990). Perceived cohesion: A conceptual and empirical examination. *Social Forces*, 69(2), 479–504.

Brock, F. (n.d.). The importance of practice: Use it or lose it, *Prolificliving.com*. [Web log comment]. Retrieved from http://www.prolificliving.com/the-importance-of-practice-use-it-or-lose-it/

Bryant, A. (2016). Corner office: Tobi Lütke of shopify: Powering a team with a 'Trust Battery'. *The New York Times*, April 22. Retrieved from https://www.nytimes.com/2016/04/24/business/tobi-lutke-of-shopify-powering-a-team-with-a-trust-battery.html

Campbell, A. (2014). The power of optimism: 91 percent of entrepreneurs confident. *Small Business Trends, Economy*, February 24. Retrieved from https://smallbiztrends.com/2014/02/power-of-optimism-91-percent-entrepreneurs-confident.html

Chamorro-Premuzic, T. (2017). *The talent delusion: Why data, not intuition, is the key to unlocking human potential*. London: Piatkus.

Chao, G. T., Walz, P. M., & Gardner, P. D. (1992). Formal and informal mentorships: A comparison on mentoring functions and contrast with non-mentored counterparts. *Personnel Psychology*, 45, 619–636.

Choi, C. Q. (2011). Culture: Like humans, chimps show selfless behaviors. *LiveScience*, August 8. Retrieved from https://www.livescience.com/15451-chimps-humanlike-altruism.html

Christensen, C. M. (2016). *Competing against luck: The story of innovation and customer choice*. New York, NY: Harper Collins.

Chun, J. U., Litzky, B. E., Sosik, J. J., Bechtold, D. C., & Godshalk, V. M. (2010). Emotional intelligence and trust in formal mentoring programs. *Group & Organization Management, 35*(4), 421–455.

Clark, R. (2005). Research-tested team motivation strategies. *Performance Improvement, 44*(1), 13–16. Retrieved from http://www.cogtech.usc.edu/publications/clark_team_motivation.pdf

Coticchia, G. (2017). 'The Founder' — 6 lessons from the movie about McDonalds. [Web log comment]. *LinkedIn*, January 22. Retrieved from https://www.linkedin.com/pulse/founder6-lessons-from-movie-mcdonalds-greg-coticchia-mba-pc

Couch, G. (2010). Senior Willie Veasley, Butler's 'Shane Battier', an unsung hero in Final Four run, April 1. Retrieved from http://www.mlive.com/spartans/index.ssf/2010/04/senior_willie_veasley_butlers.html

Covey, S. M. R., & Merrill, R. R. (2008). *The speed of trust: The one thing that changes everything*. New York, NY: Free Press.

Cross, R., Ehrlich, K., Dawson, R., & Helferich, J. (2008). Managing collaboration: Improving team effectiveness through a network perspective. *California Management Review, 59*(4), 74–98.

Daft, R., & Marcic, D. (2009). *Understanding management* (6th ed.). Mason, OH: South-Western Cengage Learning.

Decety, J. (2010). The neurodevelopment of empathy in humans. *Developmental Neuroscience*, Retrieved from https://www.ncbi.nlm.nih.gov/pmc/articles/PMC3021497/

De Meuse, K. P. (2009). A comparative analysis of the Korn/Ferry T7 model with other popular team models. The Korn/Ferry Institute. Retrieved from http://www.kornferry.com/media/lominger_pdf/teamswhitepaper080409.pdf

Doyle, T. (2011). *Learner-centered teaching: Putting the research on learning into practice*. Sterling, VA: Stylus Publishing.

Duckworth, A. (2016). *Grit: The power of passion and perseverance*. New York, NY: Simon & Schuster.

Dunbar, J. P. E. (2015). Humble leadership advances team ahead of 'self'. *Air Force Special Operations Command, News, Commentaries*, May 1. Retrieved from http://www.afsoc.af.mil/News/Commentaries/Display/Article/587263/humble-leadership-advances-team-ahead-of-self/

Ebbinghaus, H. (1913). *Memory: A contribution to experimental psychology* (1850–1909). New York, NY: Teachers College, Columbia University.

Ericsson, K. A. (2006). The influence of experience and deliberate practice on the development of superior expert performance. In K. A. Ericsson, N. Charness, P. J. Feltovich, & R. R. Hoffman (Eds.), *The Cambridge handbook of expertise and expert performance* (pp. 683–703). New York, NY: Cambridge University Press.

Ericsson, K. A., Krampe, R. T., & Tesch-Römer, C. (1993). The role of deliberate practice in the acquisition of expert performance. *Psychological Review, 100*(3), 363–406.

Ericsson, K. A., Prietula, M. J., & Cokely, E. T. (2007). The making of an expert. *Harvard Business Review, 85*(7/8), 114–121.

Favale, D. (2013). Michael Jordan's unofficial guide to success in the NBA. *The Bleacher Report*, February 14. Retrieved from http://bleacherreport.com/articles/1529861-michael-jordans-unofficial-guide-to-success-in-the-nba

Feehi, A., Boateng, H., & Mensah, D. T. (2016). The effects of job satisfaction, employee commitment, workplace friendship and team culture on service recovery performance. *Management Science Letters, 6*, 713–722. Retrieved from http://www.growingscience.com/msl/Vol6/msl_2016_53.pdf

Formichelli, L. (2016). The spirit of in-house competition. *FSR Magazine*, October, Retrieved from https://www.foodnewsfeed.com/fsr/chain-restaurants/spirit-house-competition

Gallo, C. (2012). Leadership: 5 reasons why optimists make better leaders. *Forbes*, August 8. Retrieved from https://www.forbes.com/sites/carminegallo/2012/08/08/5-reasons-why-optimists-make-better-leaders/#4c3b0f1c4e07

Gallup.com. (n.d.). The Gallup Q12 Index. Retrieved from http://www.
goalbusters.net/uploads/2/2/0/4/22040464/gallup_q12.pdf

Ghete, A. (2004). Southwest Airlines: From benchmarking to benchmarked.
Performance Magazine, October 2. Retrieved from http://www.performance-
magazine.org/southwest-airlines-from-benchmarking-to-benchmarked/

Goleman, D. (1995). *Emotional intelligence*. New York, NY: Bantam
Books.

Goleman, D. (2013). *Focus: The hidden driver of excellence*. New York,
NY: Harper Collins.

Graham, V. (2008). How to overcome arrogance. Retrieved from https://
insights.inneractiveconsulting.com/how-to-overcome-arrogance/

Greenberg, M. H., & Arakawa, D. (2006). *Optimistic managers & their
influence on productivity & employee engagement in a technology organization*. Retrieved from http://repository.upenn.edu/cgi/viewcontent.cgi?article=
1003&context=mapp_capstone

Greenleaf, R. K. (1970). The servant as leader. [PDF document]. Retrieved
from https://www.essr.net/~jafundo/mestrado_material_itgjkhnld/IV/Lideran
%C3%A7as/The%20Servant%20as%20Leader.pdf

Guest, D. (2017). Emotional management: The impact of negativity on team
performance. Retrieved from http://davidguest.com.au/buildingbusinesses/
team/emotional-management-the-impact-of-negativity-on-team-performance/

Guzzo, R. A., & Salas, E. (1995). *Team effectiveness and decision making in
organizations*. San Francisco, CA: Jossey-Bass.

Hallowell, E. M. (2015). *Driven to distraction at work: How to focus and
be more productive*. Boston, MA: Harvard Business Review Press.

Hamel, G. (n.d.). *The heart of innovation*. [Web log comment]. Retrieved
from http://www.garyhamel.com/blog/heart-innovation

Handfield, D., Lunder, K., Renner, J., Ryder, A. (Producers), & Hancock,
J. L. (Director). (2016). *The Founder* [Motion Picture]. United States:
FilmNation Entertainment, The Combine, Faliro House Productions.

Hanson, B. (n.d.). Coach athlete relationships matter (Canadian Olympic
Study). *Athlete Assessments*. Retrieved from http://athleteassessments.com/
COACH-ATHLETE-RELATIONSHIPS-OLYMPIC-STUDY/

Harvard Business Review. (2004). *Coaching and mentoring: How to develop top talent and achieve higher performance*. Boston, MA: Harvard Business School Publishing.

Hein, J. F. (n.d.). The Butler way. *American Outlook*. Retrieved from http://www.americanoutlook.org/the-butler-way.html

Hill, L., & Lineback, K. (2011). The fundamental purpose of a team. *Harvard Business Review*. Retrieved from https://hbr.org/2011/07/the-funda-mental-purpose-of-you.html

Hogg, M. A. (1992). *The social psychology of group cohesiveness*. New York, NY: New York University Press.

Hughes, V. (2014). Where do new ideas come from. *Phenomina: A Science Salon*, June 18. Retrieved from http://phenomena.nationalgeographic.com/2014/06/18/where-do-new-ideas-come-from/

Investopedia. (n.d.). 5 businesses that started during a recession. Retrieved from http://www.investopedia.com/slide-show/recession-businesses/?article=1

Janis, I. L. (1972). *Victims of Groupthink: A psychological study of foreign-policy decisions and fiascoes*. New York, NY: Houghton Mifflin Company.

Janis, I. L. (2014). *Crucial decisions: Leadership in policymaking and crisis management*. New York, NY: The Free Press.

Kelley, R. E. (1988). Leadership: In praise of followers. *Harvard Business Review*, November. Retrieved from https://hbr.org/1988/11/in-praise-of-followers

Kouzes, J. M., & Posner, B. Z. (2011). *Credibility: How leaders gain and lose it, why people demand it*. San Francisco, CA: Jossey-Bass.

Lee, J., & Ok, C. (2011). Effects of workplace friendship on employee job satisfaction, organizational citizenship behavior, turnover intention, absenteeism, and task performance, January. Paper presented at UMass Amherst Graduate Student Research Conference in Hospitality and Tourism, Amherst, MA. Retrieved from http://scholarworks.umass.edu/cgi/viewcontent.cgi?article=1053&context=gradconf_hospitality

Leib, J. (2010). Southwest Airlines hustles to reduce turnaround times. *The Denver Post*, September 25. Retrieved from http://www. denverpost.com/2010/09/25/southwest-airlines-hustles-to-reduce-turn-around-times/

Leichman, A. K. (2016). How to build an emergency field hospital in 12 hours. *Israel 21c: Uncovering Israel*, April 6. Retrieved from https://www. israel21c.org/how-to-build-an-emergency-field-hospital-in-12-hours/

Leinbach-Reyhle, N. (2014). Shedding hierarchy: Could Zappos be setting an innovative trend? *Forbes*, July 15. Retrieved from https://www.forbes. com/sites/nicoleleinbachreyhle/2014/07/15/shedding-hierarchy-could-zappos-be-setting-an-innvoative-trend/#2af58e1c26f4

Lewis, M. (2009). The no-stats All-Star. *The New York Times Magazine*, February 13. Retrieved from http://www.nytimes.com/2009/02/15/magazine/15Battier-t.html?mcubz=0

Lieberman, P. (1994). *Uniquely human: The evolution of speech, thought and selfless behavior* (3rd ed.). Cambridge, MA: Harvard University Press.

Luthans, F., Avey, J. B., Avolio, B. J., & Peterson, S. J. (2010). The development and resulting performance impact of positive psychological capital. *Human Resource Development Quarterly*, 22(1), 41–67.

Luthans, R., Youssef, C. M., & Avolio, B. J. (2007). *Psychological capital: Developing the human competitive edge*. Oxford: Oxford University Press.

Management Mentors. (n.d.). The differences between coaching and mentoring. Retrieved from http://www.management-mentors.com/resources/coaching-mentoring-differences

Mankins, M. (2013). Organizational culture: The defining elements of a winning culture. *Harvard Business Review*, December 19. Retrieved from https://hbr.org/2013/12/the-definitive-elements-of-a-winning-culture

Mankins, M., & Garton, E. (2017). Managing organizations: How spotify balances employee autonomy and accountability. *Harvard Business Review*, February 9. Retrieved from https://hbr.org/2017/02/how-spotify-balances-employee-autonomy-and-accountability

Mayer, R., Davis, J., & Schoorman, F. (1995). An integrative model of organizational trust. *The Academy of Management Review, 20*(3), 709–734. Retrieved from http://www.jstor.org/stable/258792

McCauley, C. D., & Douglas, C. A. (2004). Developmental relationships. In C. D. McCauley & V. E. Van Velsor (Eds.), *Center for creative leadership handbook of leadership development*. Chichester, Jossey-Bass

McClelland, D. C. (1953). *The achievement motive*. New York, NY: Appleton-Century-Crofts.

McCord, P. (2014). Human resource management: How Netflix reinvented HR. *Harvard Business Review*. Retrieved from https://hbr.org/2014/01/how-netflix-reinvented-hr

Mehlenbacher, B. (2002). *Communication disasters* [web page]. Lessons Online Web site. Retrieved from: http://www4.ncsu.edu/~brad_m/teaching/eng%20331/Lessons/communication.html

Mintzberg, H. (2005). *Managers not MBAs: A hard look at the soft practice of managing and management development*. Oakland, CA: Berrett-Koehler Publishers.

Molnau, D. (2017). High-performance teams: Understanding team cohesiveness. *SixSigma*. Retrieved from https://www.isixsigma.com/implementation/teams/high-performance-teams-understanding-team-cohesiveness/

Murre, J. M. J., & Dros, J. (2015). Replication and analysis of Ebbinghaus' forgetting curve. *PLoS One, 10*(7), e0120644. Retrieved from https://www.ncbi.nlm.nih.gov/pmc/articles/PMC4492928/

NASCAR.com. (2015). The anatomy of a pit stop. January 5. Retrieved from http://www.nascar.com/en_us/monster-energy-nascar-cup-series/nascar-nation/nascar-edu/nascar-basic/pit-stop.html

Neville, M. (Director). (2015). *The Music of Strangers* [Motion Picture]. United States of America: Tremolo Productions in association with Participant Media.

Newman, R. (2010). Money: 10 great companies that lost their edge. *U.S. News and World Report*, August 19. Retrieved from https://money.usnews.com/money/blogs/flowchart/2010/08/19/10-great-companies-that-lost-their-edge

Okasha, S. (2013). Biological altruism. In E. N. Zalta (Ed.). *The Stanford encyclopedia of philosophy*. Retrieved from https://plato.stanford.edu/archives/fall2013/entries/altruism-biological/

Onyx Solar. (n.d.a). Photovoltaic glass for buildings. Retrieved from http://www.onyxsolar.com/

Onyx Solar. (n.d.b). Committee of wise people. Retrieved from http://www.onyxsolar.com/wise-people-committee.html

Partners in Performance Excellence, Catalyst for Success. (n.d.). Baldrige framework and value system. Retrieved from http://partnerspex.org/pipex/baldrige_framework.ashx

PCA Development Zone®, Resource Center. (n.d.). Brad Stevens: sports can teach kids the world is bigger than they are [Video File].Retrieved from http://devzone.positivecoach.org/resource/video/brad-stevenssports-can-teach-kids-world-bigger-they-are

Peale, N. V. (2003). *The power of positive thinking*. New York, NY: Touchstone.

Pervez, M. A. (2010). Impact of emotions on employee's job performance: An evidence from organizations of Pakistan. *International Journal of Sustainable Development, 1*(5), 11–16.

Peters, T., & Waterman, R. (1982). *In search of excellence: Lessons from America's best-run companies* (1st ed.). New York, NY: Harper & Row.

Polya, G. (1973). *How to solve it: A new aspect of mathematical method* (2nd ed.). Princeton, NJ: Princeton University Press.

Popik, B. (2012). Getting good players is easy: getting them to play together is the hard part, November 29. [Web log comment]. Retrieved from http://www.barrypopik.com/index.php/new_york_city/entry/getting_good_players_is_easy_getting_them_to_play_together_is_the_hard_part

Powell, C. (2002). *The leadership secrets of Colin Powell*. New York, NY: McGraw-Hill Education.

Powell, M. (2017). The Golden State Warriors are simply too great. *New York Times*, June 5. Retrieved from https://www.nytimes.com/2017/06/05/sports/basketball/warriors-cavaliers-nba-finals-kevin-durant.html

Rath, T. (2007). *Strengths finder 2.0*. New York, NY: Gallup Press.

Rath, T. (2015). *Are you fully charged?: The 3 keys to energizing your work and life*. California, SA: Silicon Guild.

Ross, J. A. (2005). Team camaraderie: Can you have too much? *Harvard Management, Update, 10*(11), 3–4.

Sacramento State. (n.d.). Statement of human rights principles. Retrieved from http://www.csus.edu/indiv/m/merlinos/enron.html

Salas, E., DiazGranados, D., Klein, C., Burke, C. S., Stagl, K. C., Goodwin, G. F., ... Halpin, S. M. (2008). Does team training improve team performance? A meta-analysis. *Human Factors: The Journal of the Human Factors and Ergonomics Society, 50*(6), 903–933. Retrieved from http://journals.sagepub.com/doi/abs/10.1518/001872008X375009

Salas, E., Rozell, D., Mullen, B., & Driskell, J. E. (1999). The effect of team building on performance: An integration. *Small Group Research, 30*, 309–329.

Senge, P. M. (2006). *The fifth discipline: The art & practice of the learning Organization*. New York, NY: Doubleday.

Servant Leadership Institute. (n.d.). What is servant leadership. Retrieved from https://www.servantleadershipinstitute.com/what-is-servantleadership-1/

Smallwood, N., & Ulrich, D. (2004). Accounting: Capitalizing on capabilities. *Harvard Business Review*, June. Retrieved from https://hbr.org/2004/06/capitalizing-on-capabilities

Smith, A. (1776). *An inquiry into the nature and causes of the wealth of nations (1723–1790)*. London: W. Strahan and T. Cadell.

Sterling, K. [sterling8513]. (2010). *Ronald Nored interview* [Video File], October 13. Retrieved from https://www.youtube.com/watch?v=ipDrWnj4YFY

Strauss, K. (2016). Leadership: Top companies most beloved by their employees in 2016. *Forbes*, May 10. Retrieved from https://www.forbes.com/sites/karstenstrauss/2016/05/10/top-companies-most-beloved-by-their-employees-in-2016/#6b4915e1358b

Taylor, J. (2013). Build a high-performing sports team culture. *Psychology Today*, July 29. Retrieved from https://www.psychologytoday.com/blog/the-power-prime/201307/build-positive-and-high-performing-sports-team-culture

Taylor, J. (2015). You won't find athletic success without 'The Grind.' *HuffPost, The Blog*, September 16. Retrieved from http://www.huffington-post.com/dr-jim-taylor/you-wont-find-athletic-su_b_8147666.html

Team Builders Plus. (n.d.). Accountability a sticky subject for teams. Retrieved from http://teambuildersplus.com/articles/accountability-stickysub-ject-for-teams

The Engineer. (2006). The Space Shuttle Challenger disaster. Retrieved from https://www.engineering.com/Library/ArticlesPage/tabid/85/ArticleID/170/The-Space-Shuttle-Challenger-Disaster.aspx

"The *Space Shuttle Challenger* disaster: a study in organizational ethics." (n.d.). [PDF document]. Retrieved from https://www.google.com/url?sa=t&rct=j&q=&esrc=s&source=web&cd=1&cad=rja&uact=8&ved=0ahUKEwjVtse49PTVAhXmwlQKHaCGBoIQFggoMAA&url=http%3A%2F%2Fpirate.shu.edu%2F~mckenndo%2Fpdfs%2FThe%2520Space%2520Shuttle%2520Challenger%2520Disaster.pdf&usg=AFQjCNGpfVu3yAD2dthN6X4uUZYL4nRo_A

Thompson, S., & McKelvy, E. (2007). Shared vision, team learning, and professional learning communities. *Middle Ground, 10*(3), 12–14. Retrieved from http://files.eric.ed.gov/fulltext/ED497108.pdf

Walker, S. (2017). *The captain class: The hidden force that creates the world's greatest teams*. New York, NY: Random House.

Warner, F. (2002). Inside Intel's mentoring movement. *Fast Company*, March 31. Retrieved from https://www.fastcompany.com/44814/inside-intels-mentoring-movement

Weinberg, F. J., & Lankau, M. J. (2011). Formal mentoring programs: A mentor-centric and longitudinal analysis. *Journal of Management, 37*(6), 1527–1557.

Wharton@Work, Executive Education, Leadership. (2012). Lead better by knowing when to follow, September. Retrieved from https://executiveeduca-tion.wharton.upenn.edu/thought-leadership/wharton-at-work/2012/09/know-when-to-follow

Wolf, G. (1996). Business: Steve Jobs: The next insanely great thing. *Wired*, February 1. Retrieved from https://www.wired.com/1996/02/jobs-2/

Young, J. R. (2017). Stop calling college teachers 'Professors.' try 'Cognitive Coaches', says Goucher President. *EdSurge*, June 28. Retrieved from https://www.edsurge.com/news/2017-06-28-stop-calling-college-teachers-professors-try-cognitive-coaches-says-goucher-president

Yu, C. (2014). Life: Mindfulness for athletes: The secret to better performance? [Web log comment]. *Daily Burn*, June 10. Retrieved from http://dailyburn.com/life/fitness/mindfulness-techniques-athletes/

ABOUT THE AUTHORS

With over three decades of experience as a human resources executive, educator, and psychologist, **Dr. Jerry Toomer** has worked globally with individuals and teams to help them achieve their professional and personal goals in complex organizations. He has led global human resources organizations for DowDuPont in the United States and Asia (Hong Kong). As an adjunct professor and executive partner at Butler University, he has been actively involved in the development of the leadership curriculum and leadership assessment tools for the MBA program. His academic credentials include a bachelor's degree in Psychology from Wartburg College and a Ph.D. in Counseling Psychology from the University of Iowa. He was also named a Diplomate in Counseling Psychology, the field's highest professional certification and continues to be an active researcher and author in the field.

Dr. Craig Caldwell works with organizations to develop strategic direction, link implementation steps to strategy, identify organizational culture, and develop processes to bring about organizational change. Since 2007, Craig has served as an associate professor of Management in the Lacy School of Business at Butler University. He is currently the associate dean of Graduate & Professional Programs. He teaches MBA and undergraduate courses in Strategy, Leadership, and Organizational Change. He has won six teaching awards and two advising awards. His past roles include the Faculty Annual Evaluation Committee and Department Chair for Marketing & Management. Craig's research includes academic articles in *Business and Society, Journal of Leadership & Organizational Studies, The Monitor, Business and Society Review, Management Accounting Quarterly,* and *Journal of Corporate Citizenship*. He holds a doctorate from the University of Pittsburgh, an MBA from Virginia Tech, and a BA from Anderson University.

Dr. Steve Weitzenkorn is committed to helping people and organizations achieve their aspirations. Steve holds a Ph.D. in Human Learning and Organizational Behavior. He has been an organizational adviser and strategy consultant for over 25 years, working with multinational corporations, local companies, educational institutions, and not-for-profit organizations to elevate their success and formulate strategies employing a pragmatic and future-oriented approach. In addition, he has extensive experience as an instructional designer and learning innovator. His experiential and discovery learning programs have received international recognition for innovation and effectiveness. He was the lead designer for the highly engaging simulation supporting Stephen M.R. Covey's bestseller, *The Speed of Trust.* Another of his training programs won the Henkel Award for Global HR Excellence. He also received the William C. Byham Award for Innovation and Excellence in Training Technology.

Dr. Chelsea Clark is the founder and president of Chelsea Clark Consulting, LLC, a relationship research firm located in Carmel, Indianapolis. Her business assists corporate, nonprofit organizations, and academic leaders achieve their research-related objectives and solve complex social scientific questions. She is also a research associate at the Indiana University Lilly Family School of Philanthropy where she manages the School's Study of High Net Worth Philanthropy, Generosity for Life project, and Human Needs Index, among other projects. She holds a PhD in Political Psychology from the University of North Carolina at Chapel Hill.

INDEX